Praise for *Leadership Moments*

"An insightful, thought-provoking volume. These engaging stories highlight actionable principles that teach us how to lead at a higher level—with heart and soul. I couldn't recommend it more highly."

—Ken Blanchard
> Co-author, *The One Minute Manager*® and *Leading at a Higher Level*

"A wise person learns from experience—a wiser person learns from someone else's experience. Read this book and learn from some amazing experiences!"

— Marshall Goldsmith, Ph.D.
> Co-editor, *The Leader of the Future*
> Names by *Forbes* as one of five top executive coaches

"There are watershed events in all our lives that send us on a new trajectory. This is an outstanding compilation of such moments. Best of all, it is written with such deep insight that we can all gain from it."

—Jack Zenger, D.B.A.
> CEO, Zenger-Folkman
> Co-author, *The Extraordinary Leader*

"A no-nonsense primer on how to lead with conviction in a world of uncertainty."

— Hon. Rod Diridon,
> Executive Director, Mineta Transportation Institute

Praise for *Leadership Moments*

"Full of spirit, this book inspires readers to develop their own leadership presence through sustainable values and a systems perspective. One of the best leadership books I have read and among the few I recommend to my clients and students."

—Prasad Kaipa, Ph.D.
   CEO, The Kaipa Group
   Council of Trustees, Society for Organizational Learning

"Compelling stories of courage and leadership, full of candid, behind-the-scenes details."

— Joyce Osland, Ph.D.
   Lucas Endowed Professor of Global Leadership, San Jose State University

"These lessons in leading change are a unique blend of theory and practice. If you like stories with morals, you'll love these narratives!"

— Brad Maihack,
   Controller, Hewlett-Packard OpenView Software Business

"Exemplary standards for leaders. Authentic, practical, and right on target! I enjoyed the book immensely."

— Dave Heagerty,
   Chairman, Coakley Heagerty

Praise for *Leadership Moments*

"A powerful and engaging book with vital leadership principles conveyed through masterful storytelling!"
—Gloria Abe, D.M., SPHR
Co-founder, Tyson Leadership College, Tyson Foods, Inc.

"...unique personal perspectives on how, by coming face to face with major life-changing dilemmas, we can provide effective leadership to others."
—Gary Silver, M.D.
Biotech Strategy Associates

"These stories of leadership in the face of adversity are an inspiration to all who strive to move their organizations forward."
—Deborah Ludewig, J.D.
Partner, Kirkpatrick, Lockhart, Nicholson and Graham

"Couldn't put it down until I finished—a must read for every aspiring leader!"
—Ed Cheng, M.D., Ph.D.
Biometric security and e-health pioneer

LEADERSHIP MOMENTS

Turning Points that Changed Lives and Organizations

Peter Amato • Gary Bodam • Martin J. Boyle • Harold Coleman

Jon Corey • Arthur L. Jue • Ronald Lesniak • John Lohre

Peter and Monika Ressler • Carolyn Salerno

Edited by Claire Gerus

Introduction by Rick Brydges

LEADERSHIP MOMENTS
Turning Points that Changed Lives and Organizations

Cover Design by Bill Greaves, Concept West

Note for Librarians: A cataloguing record for this book is available from Library and Archives
Canada at www.collectionscanada.ca/amicus/index-e.html
ISBN 1-4120-9964-1

Printed in Victoria, BC, Canada. Printed on paper with minimum 30% recycled fibre.
Trafford's print shop runs on "green energy" from solar, wind and other environmentally-friendly power sources.

Offices in Canada, USA, Ireland and UK

Book sales for North America and international:
Trafford Publishing, 6E–2333 Government St.,
Victoria, BC V8T 4P4 CANADA
phone 250 383 6864 (toll-free 1 888 232 4444)
fax 250 383 6804; email to orders@trafford.com
Book sales in Europe:
Trafford Publishing (UK) Limited, 9 Park End Street, 2nd Floor
Oxford, UK OX1 1HH UNITED KINGDOM
phone +44 (0)1865 722 113 (local rate 0845 230 9601)
facsimile +44 (0)1865 722 868; info.uk@trafford.com
Order online at:
trafford.com/06-1721

10 9 8 7 6 5 4

To the spark of leadership greatness in everyone

Acknowledgments

Thurgood Marshall said, "None of us has gotten where we are solely by pulling ourselves up from our own bootstraps. We got here because somebody . . . helped us."

When this work was conceived, little did we realize the effort and collaboration that would be required, but what transpired was nothing short of miraculous. It became a true labor of love. Along the way, we received tremendous help and assistance, for which we are extremely grateful.

A special thanks to each of the co-authors for their tenacity in sticking with the project and for their tremendous generosity and openness in sharing their experiences, expertise, and wisdom. Their enthusiasm, encouragement, responsiveness, and feedback—not to mention their incredible stories—were a constant inspiration to press forward with the book.

Many thanks to ARC Leadership Group, Inc. for coordinating

the manuscript. We would never have made it to the finish line without their sponsorship, confidence in the value of this work, and timely guidance along the way. In addition, our warm appreciation to Trafford for their publishing assistance and to Bill Greaves of Concept West for the book layout and design.

We are also indebted to literary consultant Barbara Stahura for her wonderful sense of style and structure and to Jean Fuller for making early connections that blossomed into rich and rewarding associations. Likewise, a plethora of friends, coaches, family members, and colleagues devoted time, energy, and insight into making this endeavor a reality. Their hours of selfless assistance reflected leadership at its finest. To all, a sincere thanks.

Claire Gerus, Editor
August, 2006

Table of Contents

Introduction
Rick Brydges   1

1. Bucking the System:
Conviction in the Face of Resistance
Martin J. Boyle   7

2. Restoring Honor to Business:
Ethics in the Pursuit of Profit
Peter and Monika Ressler   19

3. Staying Cool:
Communicating Effectively Under Stress
Gary Bodam   33

4. Surviving in the Financial Services Jungle:
Constancy Amid Chaos
John Lohre   41

5.*Unveiling the Leader Within:*
The Power of Intentional Leadership
Peter Amato   59

6.*Practicing Spirit-centered Leadership:*
Lessons from a Corporate Layoff
Arthur L. Jue   69

7.*Courage Under Fire:*
Standing Firm Despite Fear
Jon M. Corey   91

8.*Creating an A-Team:*
The Challenge of Raising the Bar
Harold D. Coleman   105

9.*Rebuilding After Tragedy:*
How One Company Survived 9/11
Ronald Lesniak   119

10.*Risking It All:*
The Power of Corporate and Community Partnership
Carolyn Salerno   131

Biographies   145

End Notes   157

Introduction

Rick Brydges

General Peter Schoomaker, Commander-in-Chief of the U.S. Special Operations Command, once said that everyone needs to learn how to be a leader.[1] This profound declaration was born of an urgency to embrace the ever-increasing speed of change and complexity in our postmodern world. And it underscores our challenge in business and institutions of the 21st Century.

Yet, a leadership void persists today, requiring new and innovative solutions. We can no longer afford to rely on the top-down, command-and-control leadership lexicons that dominated the Industrial Era. We must rise to the occasion by filling this leadership vacuum with practices that prepare us for defining moments in our lives, whenever and wherever they arise.

But learning exactly *how* to seize leadership moments is another question. Renowned authors, Noel Tichy and Warren Bennis, contend that good leadership is about making sound judgments in the moment of truth.[2] Such judgments can be improved as we share *teachable leadership points of view*; that is, stories with leadership wisdom born of personal experiences.

For instance, anyone who remembers a moment when his or her life suddenly turned an extraordinary corner and required an unprecedented leap of faith will appreciate the raw courage that leap evoked. When such turning points revealed an opportunity to lead others through times of crisis, an incontrovertible awareness dawned that nothing would ever be the same again. Such is the sense of "teachableness" brought to life through the ten stories in this collection, *Leadership Moments: Turning Points that Changed Lives and Organizations.*

Each of the stories you are about to read covers a wide range of situations and speaks to individuals with every level of business experience. Every situation in this book—from CEO Ron Lesniak's challenge to resurrect his company in the turbulent aftermath of 9/11, to Jon Corey's lessons in corporate survival learned during a wartime assault in Vietnam, to Arthur Jue's experience facing an unexpected downsizing at a beleaguered IBM—represents a pivotal turning point best characterized as a "baptism by fire." From the confluence of events, stronger leaders emerged, bringing new insights to organizations and a greater appreciation for the dynamic nature of leadership.

As each story attests, the potential for leadership is not limited to a predetermined elite group at the top: it resides in us all. The test of our leadership capability occurs when opportunity meets preparedness—when one turns the corner, recognizes the challenge, and is able to say, "I'm in!" Opportunities arise daily to push beyond our previous limits. It matters not whether we are veteran managers working with vexing business issues or new recruits facing complicated corporate cultures—everyone can be a leader.

As you read these stories, we hope they will inspire you to look beyond the immediate dynamics of your own situation and see your leadership challenges as *turning points* that could potentially yield powerful transformational changes.

The Birth of *Leadership Moments*

In our intention to "get this book right," we deliberately decided to focus on "leadership in the trenches." We wanted to concentrate on practical leadership applications instead of untested ivory-tower theories. So, we screened and selected a diverse cross-section of authors, asking each to write a personal essay describing how he or she faced a teachable leadership moment.

We also asked the authors to capture the gravity of their turning points by detailing the outcomes, consequences, and lessons that ultimately elicited a new sense of leadership empowerment. The result was a rich collage of diverse experiences that demonstrated effective leadership, usually under intense pressure.

From Marty Boyle's opening account of doing the right thing, no matter the personal consequences, through the final account of Carolyn Salerno's influence in getting a major corporation to step up and address a societal need, each story in this series highlights an opportunity—usually unsought and at some peril or risk—to seize upon a *leadership moment*, a window in which converging circumstances stimulated the exercise of effectual leadership.

As we compiled the individual accounts, we noted that at least three critical elements had to coalesce in order to facilitate a leadership moment: (a) a recognition of the opportunity itself; (b) a willingness to respond by making commitments; and (c) an openness to personal learning and growth, regardless of the consequences.

For example, John Lohre, Gary Bodam, and Harold Coleman found themselves dealing with making the appropriate response. John did so through consistency and patience amid political back-stabbing, Gary demonstrated self-mastery in overcoming anger, and Harold found the courage to champion change by re-engineering faulty processes.

In the case of Peter and Monika Ressler, the challenge was to violate long-held taboos in speaking of spirituality amid Wall Street's culture of greed and the quest for profit at all costs. Nevertheless, despite the diversity of each story, the accounts merged nicely to create complementary leadership paradigms and approaches.

Leadership Lessons and Themes

While each of the experiences in this book arose from a unique set of circumstances, several common leadership themes emerged. For example, each story portrayed leadership as the antecedent to transformational change, both personal and organizational. Also, each author advanced the idea that leadership is about living up to our highest espoused values.

A prime example would be referencing *people* as our most important consideration and attending to the welfare and dignity of all stakeholders when it matters most: when under pressure to perform. In each case, the humanistic, spiritual aspect of leadership emerged as a common theme.

These stories also directly or indirectly challenged a number of myths surrounding leadership, such as the fallacy that "leaders are always right." They're not. Such misconceptions are a remnant of the *Great Man Theory*, which we do not necessarily endorse.

Leaders are real people, not demigods. However, effective leaders have an uncanny ability to look themselves in the mirror, envision new possibilities, and make course corrections as they go.

Each story also chronicled a leader's personal struggle to survive great socio-organizational perils: recessions, layoffs, politics, career-ism, greed, materialism, tragedy, and the list goes on. Each vignette represented real-time action research, creating a flow of learning that can aid us in discovering how leadership best works – or doesn't – for ourselves.

Before choosing to take action, each leader acceded to self-reflec-tion (even if only momentarily), then opted to move forward with decisiveness, remaining true to personal principles and substituting faith for fear. While the specific solutions were diverse, each author transcended inner and outer forces while simultaneously champion-ing change, improving performance, and creating the conditions for others to excel.

The resulting themes paint a colorful picture that will both inspire and instruct. Each lesson contributes to the premise that leadership potential exists in all of us. Indeed, leadership can be engraved in our characters through the totality of our life experiences, as evidenced by our choices and actions.

One unique example of this process is that of business leader, Peter Amato. In his case, he recognized the need to reawaken the dignity of his own spirit during a personal time of trial, leading him to a profound understanding of the connectedness between his divine nature and his physical, emotional, and social well-being. He then embarked on a journey to share this awareness with the world at large, extending his own transformation to others who sought deeper connections with spirit, whether at work or elsewhere.

As you read each story, we hope that some or all of them will resonate with you and reinforce your own leadership wisdom and experiences. In the end, none of us knows when it will be our turn to encounter that unexpected fork in the road, or the situation that will evoke the best leadership that we can offer. However, after reading these inspiring true stories, we trust that you will be better prepared to say, "I'm in!"

Rick Brydges
August, 2006

1

Bucking the System:
Conviction in the Face of Resistance

Martin J. Boyle

Few men are willing to brave the disapproval of their fellows, the censure of their colleagues, the wrath of their society. Moral courage is a rarer commodity than bravery in battle or great intelligence. Yet it is the one essential, vital quality of those who seek to change a world which yields most painfully to change. — Robert F. Kennedy[3]

I can remember the year well—it was the "best of years and the worst of years." U.S. advertising was finally allowed on Soviet TV, but then TV evangelist Jimmy Swaggart's sex scandal shook millions of viewers. The world's longest undersea tunnel was completed, but devastating fires also ripped through Yellowstone National Park. Soviet troops were finally pulled out of Afghanistan, but terrorists succeeded in exploding Pan Am Flight 103 over Lockerbie, Scotland.

The year 1988 was a high and low point for me personally as well. In the midst of local, national, and world turmoil, I would reach new plateaus of leadership by cultivating the courage to follow my inner convictions. Yet, as I painfully learned, this would occur at tremendous personal risk and financial sacrifice.

On December 7, 1988, about a month after George Bush, Sr. won the election for the U.S. Presidency, Armenia suffered two major earthquakes, measuring 6.9 and 5.8 respectively on the Richter scale. Although the former U.S.S.R. territory was small, it was home to more than 11 million people and 400,000-plus children.

The earthquake's toll was high. More than 70% of all buildings in Armenia were destroyed, up to 100,000 people were killed, and more than half a million people were left homeless. The entire territory was devastated. In response, an unprecedented worldwide relief effort ensued, involving 111 countries, scores of international agencies, and countless volunteer workers.[4]

In one of his first tasks as President-Elect, George Bush, Sr. decided to have his son, Jeb, accompany an aircraft bound for Armenia loaded with emergency supplies collected by various charitable organizations.

At the time, I was the district security manager for a top-gun team of security personnel in my company. The company I worked for had volunteered one of its cargo-carrying DC-8 aircraft to transport these supplies along with representatives of the U.S. envoy to Armenia and other distinguished dignitaries. Needless to say, I was proud of my company's efforts to exercise good corporate citizenship.

I naturally assumed that this high-profile excursion would require the highest level of protective measures to ensure the safety of the dignitaries and the U.S. envoy. However, decisions that I regarded as common sense turned out to be an annoying expense to my local company leaders.

External Conflict, Internal Resolve

Our company's senior management knew that physical security had to be an essential component of this crucial humanitarian mission, and they wanted the best that could be provided. However, my immediate manager felt that such high security measures would be an utter waste of funds, personnel, and resources.

This unexpected gridlock created consternation among the management chain, and the urgency of the situation grew. In frustration, corporate security finally decided to bypass the regional channels and contacted me directly. They asked me to help spearhead the entire security effort for the relief operation, and I was happy to oblige.

Our district was one of sixty-three across the U.S., so being considered for this opportunity was quite an honor. It validated our solid internal reputation and our ability to get the job done. However, this corporate request also represented a highly unusual breach of protocol.

Perhaps I should offer some background. I have been in the security business for over 32 years, during which I've overseen security for numerous corporations, including many of the Fortune 500. I've also been bodyguard for some of the world's highest net-worth individuals—movie stars, rock stars, beauty queens, celebrities, politicians, billionaires, and a host of other high-and-low-profile notables.

In this environment, due to the nature of our work, security professionals have to develop a special relationship of trust with our clients. After all, we are responsible for their physical and financial well-being, so there's little room for error.

Consequently, "rules of engagement" matter—they can spell life or death. For security professionals, the chain of command is everything, and obeying formal protocol with exactness is an unwritten law of survival.

The fact that our corporate security team would breach protocol and make a direct request to me emphasized the seriousness of the mission. I felt that a tremendous trust had been placed in our district security team, and I vowed that, just as we had never failed the company in the past, we wouldn't fail it this time, either.

Along with my technical expertise, however, I was also familiar with the ugly face of corporate politics. While many of my superiors had been dedicated to advancing the organization, I had also worked for leaders who were driven by greed, ambition, and the desire for power and control. Such was the case during the Armenia mission.

My manager, who opposed participation in the Armenia campaign, became suspicious of my intentions, especially when he discovered that I had been contacted directly by the "corporate stiffs." This chain of events created friction and tension for my team and me.

Nevertheless, I couldn't deny my desire to serve. I felt deep compassion for the citizens of Armenia and wanted to do the right thing. I even sent a personal check to the United Nations Armenian representative to help purchase additional relief supplies. Now, I quietly resolved to align with corporate security and to dive into the project.

Encountering Resistance, Making a Stand

Once I decided to throw my support behind corporate and accept the mission, I immediately called a planning session with my security agents and invited my manager to attend. During the meeting, I shared our corporate vision, the importance of the mission, and the target outcome.

I also explained that, in addition to its humanitarian purpose, the mission offered us an opportunity to represent our company, our industry, and our country in a highly visible manner on the international scene. This was a rare opportunity for those of us who usually provided security in the shadow of anonymity.

I also reassured my boss that our involvement would incur little, if any, costs beyond our team's normal budget allocation. But to my surprise and disappointment, my words fell on deaf ears. At the end of the meeting, my boss announced that our team would *not* participate in a "dog-and-pony-show" simply because someone at corporate had a "bleeding heart."

The room was silent as my team and I struggled to understand my manager's perspective. I repeated the severity of the situation, as well as our obligation to fulfill our company's request to take on the mission.

But the more I spoke, the more belligerent my boss became, challenging upper management's sanity and my own motives in aligning with them. He even tried to embarrass me in front of my team.

To avoid further confrontation, I abruptly adjourned the meeting. Everyone emptied the room. "I need time to think," I told myself, shaken by my manager's response. Moments later, I knew what I must do.

I called another meeting with my team, this time excluding my manager. Then, I asked my team for their honest feedback. What did they think of my manager's decision and its ramifications?

I listened to the others, and finally decided it was time to make a decision. I told them I was making the commitment "here and now" to move ahead and organize the relief effort, despite my manager's edict. I also admitted that my decision was probably career-limiting (if not suicidal) and that I did not expect anyone to agree with me. I reassured my team that anyone who did not participate would not receive retribution from me.

Conversely, it was very likely that anyone who *did* assist me would incur unpleasant repercussions from my boss. To protect their anonymity, I suggested that anyone who wanted to join me in organizing security for the mission report back to my office within the hour for further instructions.

The Team Weighs In

Later, as I sat in my office, I wondered, "Will anyone come forward? Am I on my own?" I began to prepare myself to "stand alone and be vilified." I knew my boss could terminate my job, or worse, sideline the rest of my career.

But much to my surprise, after that second meeting, a steady stream of people began arriving at my office. Not only did all of my direct reports show up, but *their* direct reports came, too, including hourly administrative assistants! This overwhelming response gave me a moment's pause as I asked myself: "Am I ready to accept responsibility for an entire department possibly getting fired?"

Even though I had accepted full responsibility for my own decision and actions, I cringed at the idea of my manager taking swift retribution on everyone who opted to follow my lead. I thought of the many times in history when masses of followers suffered ignominious fates at the hands of their crazed leaders. Would this be one of those times? The potential political consequences seemed equally, if not more, dangerous than the mission itself.

However, my subordinates showed their support and eagerly offered a wealth of suggestions about how to execute the mission. My entire team committed to the assignment without a second thought about the political ramifications or personal repercussions. I repeatedly warned everyone about possible payback from my manager, but they continued to work cheerfully away at our plan.

In retrospect, I probably shouldn't have been surprised at the response from my team. A tremendous *esprit de corps* exists between "colleagues in arms" within the security industry. Healthy relationships between peers are usually based on a tight bond of trust and mutual respect. Everyone on my team knew that I would do whatever it took to secure their safety while pursuing the mission. They knew I had their best interests at heart, and each of them reciprocated in turn.

Realizing that this might be our final assignment together, my team and I began to focus on accomplishing the mission ahead. We came up with what we considered a winning strategy for a successful mission to Armenia. And we all knew that now there was no turning back.

Execution, Execution, Execution

Time was running short. We were down to five days before liftoff and still had to contact a number of sources for airport security and other logistical support. The safest travel routes had to be determined, and proactive scenario-planning had to be done. It would be a massive undertaking.

I had the team immediately start notifying the appropriate airports, and we initiated communication with other support organizations. I also concentrated on managing project costs.

Though our expenses were minor compared with the significance of the mission, I assumed that all costs would have to be absorbed by my department. Therefore, I invested tremendous time and effort calculating how to best accommodate them. Little did I realize that, at the end of the mission, headquarters would step up and absorb all of the costs themselves! There is certainly something to be said for choosing the right path and letting the consequences follow!

As the envoy embarked, our planning paid off. We were organized and well-prepared. As we assumed our positions on the runway tarmacs and in surrounding buildings, I was confident that we had left no stone unturned.

Still, the mission was no cakewalk. We endured extremely harsh conditions. I recall a study that later showed how post-traumatic stress disorder not only affected the quake victims in Armenia but the relief workers who aided them. As witnesses to the horror, our hearts went out to them.

Each of us remained on our feet for sixteen-hour shifts, and I cannot even recall eating, although I'm sure I did at some point. As the temperatures plummeted to the low twenties, our team was frequently forced to work in torrential rains and pelting ice storms. Since the campaign occurred the week before Christmas, culminating on Christmas Eve, it also inconvenienced our families at home. But despite everything, the meaning of the season made this trip all the more important for us.

Ultimately, the mission was a complete success. President Bush thanked me personally, and even the media interviews before and after the mission—usually chaotic events—went flawlessly. These were welcome rewards for my exhausted team, now physically drained after the envoy had returned home. But our hearts were full knowing that we had helped countless Armenians in crisis, and that we had successfully passed the test.

However, my ordeal had just begun. I soon learned that a political backlash awaited me, spawned by my manager's fury and my organization's apathy when it came to supporting me and my team.

Weathering the Aftermath

Immediately upon my return to the office, my boss reassigned me to the evening shift, akin to being assigned to Purgatory. Here I remained for several years. This encroached on my family time and created other tensions, but I decided to bear my punishment as stoically as possible. I had made my choice, and now I would accept the consequences.

Ironically, my manager's punitive actions actually became a double-edged sword. By placing me on night duty, he was forced to handle sensitive security matters without the benefit of my assistance or input. He also had to scramble to meet required "departmental numbers," which became extremely labor-intensive for him.

In addition to the inconveniences of time and schedule, I also suffered financially. I was passed over or given minimal raises for the next several years, and my year-end bonus came only because company policy mandated it. Still furious with me, my boss restricted my access to departmental funds, inhibiting my ability to adequately increase my employees' pay scales.

This punishment certainly strained my capacity to perform effectively, not to mention negatively affecting my long-term earning potential and upward mobility in the firm.

"What happened to corporate?" you're probably asking. "Didn't they come riding to your rescue?" To my surprise, although they had asked me to override my boss's wishes in the first place, and knew of the repercussions later visited upon me, they remained mute, refusing to intervene for several years! Apparently, while they could summon up the courage to breach corporate protocol during a "crunch," they had little stomach for doing the same on my behalf after the job was done.

My long hours laboring in an invisible corporate penalty box seemed like eons. Then, one day, somebody must have remembered me, and I was quietly transferred to a highly coveted position within Information Services.

At the time, I felt that this promotion was too little, too late, and others close to the situation seemed to agree. I considered that I had probably been promoted merely for the sake of political expediency.

On a more positive note, however, none of my people had experienced any repercussions because (a) I had taken full responsibility for the entire operation, and (b) my manager knew that my team could make or break his regular "reporting numbers." These numbers determined his compensation and future career advancement in the company. Consequently, I alone served as the sacrificial lamb.

Leadership Lessons Learned

My decision and subsequent actions to lead the mission came from my heart and my gut. I later learned that I had unknowingly followed Joseph Rost's fourfold definition of leadership by (a) influencing relationships (b) among leaders and followers (c) based on mutual purposes (d) to effect positive change.[5]

Although I found it hard to believe that anyone could resent such a purely humanitarian mission, I took comfort in knowing that my team had chosen the road of true leadership, versus the road of rote management and blind obedience.

Many of our company-trained managers had been taught about "spheres of influence," which espoused accomplishing tasks by influencing authority higher up the chain. Yet, it was never clearer to me than during the mission to Armenia that "the buck stops here." Rather than wasting time maneuvering through corporate politics or seeking approval from my boss or his peers, I had aimed for a higher purpose.

My decision to proceed was actually liberating for me. In order to do the right thing, I learned that it is sometimes preferable to ask for forgiveness later, rather than to ask for permission beforehand.

As for my team, I firmly believe that by sticking to their convictions, they were freed to perform their level best in executing our plan. It alleviated many self-defeating pressures that they might have otherwise encountered. I also learned that while following one's conscience can bring a leader into conflict with organizational inertia and resistance, the personal peace gained within is always worth it.

I recall conducting a debriefing at midnight on the final evening of the mission to discuss lessons learned. What I discovered was that everything I had ever been taught about leadership and security had come into play during the week. All of the "what-if" scenarios we had conceived had either been implemented or tested somehow. By standing ready, we were able to respond to the call.

The courage I gained from that mission to Armenia has served me well over the years. Leadership decision-making has become clearer to me in an industry where there are often large purported "gray areas." I have also learned that carrying a gun professionally does not necessarily mean that you must become callous and leave your heart behind. On the contrary, it becomes even more vital to *do the right thing*, not just to do things right.

All's Well that Ends Well

My team and I were eventually vindicated over time. In fact, my boss actually went on to take credit for the success of the operation, although everyone knew he had opposed it.

I became stronger and more trusted as a leader, and when the company asked me to coordinate security for athletes and dignitaries during the 1996 Summer Olympics in Atlanta Georgia, I was ready and willing to serve. It became one of the most exciting six weeks of my life.

Again, the endeavor was an overwhelming success, reinforcing my team's reputation and my own credibility in the nationwide security arena. Eventually, I decided to begin my own business, offering protective and counter-terrorism services to clients worldwide.

Today, I reflect upon my past experiences when confronting challenges. I've learned that nearly every praiseworthy objective faces opposition. Numerous traps, roadblocks, and frustrations tend to emerge when providing leadership in the trenches of daily organizational life.

But as my band of loyal security personnel demonstrated, even more important than overcoming hurdles and achieving goals is the realization that higher purposes and inner peace can be ours by staying true to our deepest convictions. Perhaps Theodore Roosevelt said it best when he stated:

It is not the critic who counts, not the man who points out how the strong man stumbled, or where the doer of deeds could have done them better.

The credit belongs to the man who is actually in the arena; whose face is marred by dust and sweat and blood; who strives valiantly; who errs and comes short again and again;

who knows the great enthusiasms, the great devotions, and spends himself in a worthy cause; who, at the best, knows in the end the triumph of high achievement;

and who, at the worst, if he fails, at least fails while daring greatly, so that his place shall never be with those cold and timid souls who know neither victory nor defeat.[6]

2

Restoring Honor to Business: Ethics in the Pursuit of Profit

Peter and Monika Ressler

Peter's story

A year after the September 11th attack, New York started to move forward again. The sixty foot pile of twisted steel and debris at Ground Zero had been removed. New York's former center of commerce, with connections throughout the modern world, had been reduced to sixteen acres of dirt. It looked more like an ordinary construction site than the war zone it had become.

But the enormous hole in the ground where the Twin Towers had once stood mirrored the hole in our hearts. It also represented the hole in our business during the year that had just passed.

With the removal of this physical reminder of the horror of September 11, New York's citizens, recovery workers, and businesses felt some closure to their year of pain. Now, the city's future stretched before it like a blank canvas. New Yorkers not only had to focus on rebuilding their companies, but they had to restore meaning to their lives.

As CEO of a Wall Street search firm catering to top-tier investment banks, I had been in business for twenty-one years. Yet, nothing had prepared me for this. Recession was one thing—seasoned business veterans expected economic slowdowns. But a complete meltdown by an act of horrific violence in New York City was something I had never imagined.

My focus had been on putting deals together, serving clients and developing new ones. After 9/11, I spoke to dozens of colleagues about lost friends and victims of the disaster, and we observed together how the Wall Street we had known was struggling to survive.

The year had changed me on a personal level, too. I was more circumspect, more thoughtful. Two months after the attack, I had become a volunteer for my local fire department on Long Island, New York. My friends and relatives thought I was crazy, but I needed to feel useful. Business was at a standstill for the foreseeable future, and I felt helpless standing on the sidelines.

Before volunteering, I had forged several links to the fire department. In fact, the first official casualty of the attack, Father Mychal Judge (Chaplain of the New York City fire department), was a close personal friend. Now, I felt I had to give back. Becoming a volunteer firefighter was the best way I knew how.

I spent many evenings at firehouses listening to painful stories of loss. Truly, this was a time I would never forget, and one that would launch me into a new life—and new definitions of leadership.

The World after 9/11

My wife, Monika, and I had moved our firm two years earlier to West 25th Street near Credit Suisse First Boston. We preferred this neighborhood to both downtown and midtown congestion. Before the attack, we were equidistant from our clients on Wall Street, the World Financial Center, the World Trade Center and midtown.

A few days a week, sometimes a few times a day, I would hop on the subway and meet clients in the World Trade Center. After the attack, our clients moved around the city and even out of state to New Jersey and Connecticut.

One large investment bank, with which I'd worked, was severely affected by the attack. It was located in the financial district, but had been saved from a direct hit. Now, it was struggling to recoup its losses. In the first month after 9/11, it had laid off 1,000 people, including an entire HR department with which I had worked every day for ten years. Clearly, this had a serious impact on my own business as well.

In the immediate aftermath, we did what all other businesses did. We cut costs and eliminated every conceivable expense right down to paper clips. The year 2002 was the worst in my experience since "Black Monday" in 1987. At that time, headhunting on Wall Street died a quick death until life resurfaced a year later, culminating in record profits in 1989. I hoped that 2003 would rebound similarly. Only this time, things were very different—it wasn't just business that had died, but actual people, many very dear to me.

Formerly an enthusiastic businessman, I now found that my passion for work had disappeared. My Wall Street colleagues felt the same way. One high-yield bond trader summed it up in the months after the attack, "Everything we do seems trivial now."

Monika worked with me on contract negotiations, managed all of our firm's financial needs, and oversaw investments for the company. Fortunately, she had continued to invest profits in real-estate ventures in the years prior to 9/11. These properties had been intended as long-term investments. However, it became necessary to liquidate some of them to stay afloat until the storm passed.

Destruction Comes in Many Forms

In the summer of 2002, the real-estate market was booming again, and business slowly began to recover. Yet, both retail equity markets and the institutional equity markets of our investment banking clients were suffering huge losses.

The banks were now laying off large numbers of employees and eliminating expenses, such as retained searches. Fortunately, some of our clients had large earnings from fixed-income markets to help sustain them.

We had learned that long-term business is developed by creating and keeping satisfied clients. Reputation is everything, and profits often depend on it. I had been lucky over the years—we'd developed a loyal clientele of high powered managers.

However, in 2002 a coup had been underway at the offices of one of our most valued clients. We had spent fifteen years in a close, mutually beneficial working relationship. I knew the head of every division personally. But now, the carnage of the terrorist attack was leading to more destruction as several long-standing corporate officers were pushed out of the firm.

I had been through this type of transition before. I knew that I could either choose to work with the new management or follow my previous associates to other institutions. Since these power shifts often became positive forces for change—and Wall Street is always in transition—I tried to work with the new management team.

In early 2003, I found this client a candidate to fill an asset-backed finance position. We had worked on this placement for months, a complicated process due to the volatile marketplace. We came close to filling the assignment a number of times, but the deal would always fall apart. Finally, we found a perfect fit and completed our assignment.

In the current economic climate, however, retainer payments had disappeared, and I could no longer count on guaranteed funds to cover my overhead. Confident that things would work out, I had taken this in stride, sure that I could produce the right candidate. I also knew that this client's principle finance division was hugely profitable. It would not only be able to pay the talent, but me as well. Closing the deal on this position assured us that we could avoid any further downsizing of our already reduced staff.

To my shock, however, the co-head of the desk, exercising his new authority, decided to change the terms of our contract after the search was completed.

Now, he was offering me one-third of our agreed-upon fee. "That's not our deal," I said, and referred to the contract he had signed with us months before. I also cited fee structures going back ten years.

"Take it or leave it," he said, and threatened to pull out altogether if I did not agree to his new terms. I had renegotiated contracts all the time, but *before,* not *after,* the deal was done. This man knew I would not want to jeopardize a fifteen-year client relationship. He also knew my post-9/11 business was compromised and was taking advantage of the vulnerable economic environment.

I was stunned and deeply disappointed. I had not anticipated that a long-term client would betray my trust, especially in a hugely profitable year for his company.

I couldn't help contrasting this man's actions with those of the honorable firefighters who had risked their lives for others. In stark contrast, this powerful business manager served his own personal interests at the expense of others. Would our firm survive the betrayal? Yes, of course it would. Would it change our relationship? Absolutely!

If this had been an act of economic desperation on my client's part, I would have accepted it. However, I knew that the division had reported record revenues for the year. Their profits had actually tripled! I also knew that management had reduced staff by 5,000 people, slicing any extra expenses, including my retainer fee.

These actions had resulted in a stellar year for them. One of my friends at their firm enthusiastically reported that he had been compensated with a 12 million dollar bonus over his previous year's salary of five million! Management had paid itself with a 150% salary increase over the pre-9/11, pre-layoff year.

When I informed my friend of his co-head's action, he went to bat for me and fought his colleague over our reduced fee. When that failed, my friend went to the management committee. Although he was as financially successful as his new "partner" at the firm, he had a higher ethical code. Both of us had profited handsomely from our professional relationship; yet, we had never turned our backs on each other to do so.

Unfortunately, in this new climate my friend no longer had the same power. Although he was a top producer, his authority had been diminished. In its place, the new managers had adopted a new ethical code. The firm I had worked with for almost two decades traded its "my word is my bond" motto for the mantra of "profit at any cost." Suddenly, all bets were off, and survival-of-the-fittest reigned.

Up until then, I had always operated on the honor system. I had developed a large network of trustworthy associates in the institutional debt and equity world. But the act by this new manager threw me back to my early days after graduating from Cornell.

As a rookie recruiter for a large midtown search firm, I had observed many headhunters profiting greatly by lying and cheating. They would tell clients or candidates anything they wanted to hear just to close a deal. When I had questioned a colleague about this practice, he responded, "They'll never find out." The president of the firm I worked for told me, "When I look at a candidate, I see a dollar sign across his face."

Because of such attitudes, Monika and I had struck out on our own. We knew we could seek profit and still remain ethical. One might make a killing in the short term, but it's integrity that builds the future.

I accepted the reduced fee that the new manager offered, but made a tough decision, despite the fact that we were now at the height of a deep recession. I refused to do business with him again. After all, how could I sell this firm to candidates if I didn't believe in it myself?

For years, like many of my colleagues, I had taken unscrupulous behavior in stride. I discovered that there were two types of business people: those who could be trusted and those who could not. I played hardball with those who tried to cheat and forged solid relationships with those of honor.

This incident coincided with the stream of revelations from other far more lucrative business shenanigans. Enron, WorldCom, Adelphia, Tyco, Wall Street analysts, and white shoe accounting firms were exposed as padding their own pockets at an enormous expense to others.

Something was inherently wrong. We all wanted to make money, but at what cost to one's integrity? I discussed this with my colleagues, and all of us were frustrated with excesses that were devastating markets for everyone.

The bottom line is, in the global economy, we're all connected. For example, when WorldCom declared bankruptcy, it reverberated around the world. Its CEO, a man Monika and I had never met, triggered an enormous debacle through his fraud and personal greed, destroying countless businesses and severely damaging others, including ours.

Many investment bankers were also disgusted with the outrageous antics of "star analysts" whose prosecutions made us all look bad. Rogue analysts made money for their firms any way they could. If they didn't, they were often fired, or worse, unnoticed.

Still, there were plenty of us on Wall Street and in the corporate world who didn't need to deceive anyone to make a profit. This duality ignited a fire in me. Like the firefighter I was trained to be, I needed to put this moral conflagration out.

My wife convinced me that it was time to write about this phenomenon. That decision would prove to be a turning point in our professional lives.

Monika's story

Throughout 2002, Peter was training as a probationary firefighter by night and working as a business executive by day. The two worlds were in direct contrast to each other. The brief humanitarian mood of Wall Street directly following the attack had become a fleeting memory just a year later. It was business as usual with the sharks swimming around the wounded once again. Yet, each week after attending "fire school," Peter came home with new lessons learned.

The basic firefighter code includes the concept of teamwork. Firefighters work as a unit, no matter what they do outside of work. Whether or not they like each other, in an official capacity they labor together for the same purpose. This is the foundation of their brotherhood.

One of Peter's class instructors described it like this: "You never leave without your brother. When he leaves, you leave. If he is down, you stay until you can get him out."

This concept was pounded into their brains from the earliest training. Teamwork is the heart of being a firefighter. No one takes the spotlight away from anyone else. You each have a job to do, and you perform to the best of your ability. The team's survival depends on it. If the team succeeds, so do you. That's how a firefighter measures success, by the team's accomplishment.

Our business thrived on partnership with our clients and employees. Our primary client for many years was one of the top three investment banking firms in the world. Gradually we became their exclusive search firm, working as a team with their entire organization.

Teamwork was the philosophy that had propelled them to the top of their field, and together we focused on helping them stay there. Each of us had a job to do that we performed to the best of our ability. When we did well, everyone connected with the placement looked good.

Peter came home one night from firefighting training and said he had learned the code of the firefighter: "In unity there is strength." This code mirrored the view of our primary client. We began to talk about how, if this simple concept were adopted by the rest of the business world, it could change the face of business as we knew it.

The co-head of the desk that betrayed our trust, the corporate officers being prosecuted, and the rogue analysts in the news did not understand that we were all in this together. We could either have honor in the pursuit of profit, or operate out of pure self-interest without regard for how our actions affected anyone else. The choice was ours.

Our Solution

We decided to publish a book in 2004 called, "Spiritual Capitalism: What the FDNY Taught Wall Street About Money." In the months leading to its release, Peter and I began to wonder whether its publication might negatively affect our business. Would we lose clients who didn't like our message?

By writing about corporate ethics as Wall Street headhunters, we were breaking a long-standing taboo. The common belief was that business "isn't personal." You never discussed anything personal in connection with work. Yet, we were being very candid in our book about our post- 9/11 experiences.

As publication date approached, we agonized over whether or not we should go through with it. Our business was starting to return to its pre-9/11 levels. Why would we want to "rock the boat" after everything we had been through these past few years?

"Have we lost our sanity?" "What if our clients feel betrayed because we broke the taboo of never mixing our personal and business lives?" "Will they think we've become soft and lost our competitive drive?"

All these questions loomed before us.

The more we questioned ourselves, the more we realized that our book was a huge risk to our livelihood and the future of our firm. We had built our business on discretion. We served quietly behind the scenes catering to our clients' needs. We never advertised. All of our business was developed via referrals. We never discussed religion, spirituality, or shared any of our personal lives with business associates. It was an unspoken understanding that these topics were separated from Wall Street deal-making.

Finding Courage

Finally, as the memories kept surfacing of those who had been lost and those who were still suffering, we remembered how it was unity that had saved us. We read daily about new business scandals and saw how the selfishness of a few created hardship for tens of millions. Inspired by the courage of firefighters who helped to rebuild our city, we knew this had to be said, and we might as well be the ones to say it.

It was a scary time, but we decided to go for it. In light of post-9/11, the loss of life, the great human tragedy we had witnessed, and the unbridled greed that created such deep suffering, we couldn't stand by as spectators any longer.

The words "in unity there is strength" echoed in our minds. We wondered how many others were feeling the same way. Would the words in our book help stimulate a more ethical pursuit of profit? Was "capitalism with a conscience" worth writing about at the risk of shattering our insulated, sheltered world?

We would never find out if we didn't try. As we took the greatest risk of our careers, our personal discomfort became secondary to the greater good. It was no longer going to be "business as usual."

We put our own needs aside, and like the firefighters who moved us so deeply, we faced our fears and moved forward with the publication of "Spiritual Capitalism."

Peter's story
A Brave New World

We had hoped there were other people in business who felt as we did, and it turned out that we were right. Many business people thanked us for writing the book, encouraged that someone from a cutthroat business environment like Wall Street spoke about finding purpose in the pursuit of profit.

Others said they never thought of business as being either personal or a service to others. Our book shifted the way they thought about their livelihoods. Still others felt a new connection between themselves, their customers, clients, co-workers, employers, and employees.

As we began doing radio and television interviews, book signings and talks, we struck a responsive chord in many, many people. After a lecture in St Louis, Missouri, the event organizer said, "I have never thought about how my job touched others before. I always thought it was just a way to put food on the table. I will never look at my work the same way again."

A colleague told us how he passed a construction crew on the road every day while driving to work. He cursed them under his breath for slowing traffic until he read our chapter on the spiritual nature of work. Now he drives by and silently thanks them for being there.

Building a Network

For Monika and me, however, the real litmus test came from Wall Street itself. Our fears fell away as we received overwhelming support. For example, New Jersey Senator Jon Corzine, former Chair of Goldman Sachs, endorsed our book and said: "Spirituality and good business practices can go hand in hand."

Martin Shafiroff, listed by Barron's as America's number one retail broker, gave another endorsement, and the chair of one of the world's top three mutual funds bought fifty copies for his sales people.

The managing director of the debt and equity division of a medium-sized investment bank bought books for every employee, while the owner of a two billion dollar hedge fund began a dialogue with us about business ethics. At a recent conference in New York, a former Morgan Stanley marketing director called our book, "a landmark on Wall Street."

These reactions from the Street encouraged us to continue. We realized that others were hungry for these changes, and we began developing seminars for corporations, investment banks, and financial institutions on "how to inspire productivity and increase profit with the principles of Spiritual Capitalism."

What happened to our search business? It's flourishing with new vigor! We had stopped working with the investment bank that changed management and subsequently its ethics code. However, we got calls from them for months afterward, trying to convince us to continue representing them. But they still refused to honor their contract, so we declined their offer.

Over time, all the former managers and our clients have moved to other investment banks, commercial banks, and hedge funds. As a result, after a few difficult years following September 11th, our business has expanded to other institutions. Our fees are the same. The search business is still our primary focus, and we continue to represent our clients to the best of our ability. The concepts of "Spiritual Capitalism" inspired by the post-9/11 Wall Street have led to more referrals than ever before.

Monika's story
Lessons Learned

More than anything, we learned that every leadership challenge we face in business is an opportunity for transformation. If we play it safe, the outcome is fairly predictable. When we take the risks that we feel in our gut are valuable, the results can be greater than we ever imagined. Before September 11th, we were comfortable in our safe, protected world as Wall Street search consultants. Yet our safety was blown apart by circumstances beyond our control. Leadership in business, as in life, is affected by unpredictable forces.

Whether it is a hurricane or terrorism, an act of God or an act of man, we have to adapt to the changes in our lives and our business or we cannot survive. Change is the one constant in life, and business is no exception.

After our hearts were broken by the tragedy of September 11th, we wondered how we could ever find passion for work again. We saw the worst of humanity on that day. *The attack affected our firm and our lives very personally. We came close to losing everything. Others did lose everything.*

Yet in the midst of all the misery that surrounded us, we also witnessed the best of humanity. The business community in New York formed a team, inspired by the New York firefighters, that was the key to our recovery. The subsequent business scandals that occurred in the years after the attack and reverberated throughout the nation's economy and continue today are reminders of a call to action. The short-sighted self-interest of a select few threatens the safety and comfort of us all.

"In unity there is strength." We have seen the truth of this statement both through our Wall Street experiences and the heroic leadership of the New York firefighters. Teamwork is the thing that pulls us together. Indifferent self-interest and unbridled greed are the things that tear us apart.

In business, it is possible to combine profit with a higher purpose. We know many hugely successful businesses and individuals who have done just that. We have chosen to write and talk about it. We do so with the hunch that there are many like-minded business leaders out there. Leadership is strengthened or broken by the challenges we face. Inspired by the sacrifices of our firefighters, we pushed past our fears and found courage we did not know we had. In the process, we discovered a new passion and enthusiasm for our work.

By choosing to use our greatest challenge as an opportunity to transform ourselves and our business, the rewards have been greater than we could have possibly imagined.

3

Staying Cool: Communicating Effectively Under Stress

Gary Bodam

When Mount St. Helens erupted in 1980, I watched the televised reports, fascinated by the fury that forcibly hurled the fire, smoke, cinders, and lava out of the bowels of the mountain and hundreds of feet into the air. The ensuing volcanic cloud, a blowtorch of debris and ashes, was traveling over 200 miles per hour down the side of the mountain.

The extreme heat of the rocks and gas inside, generally between 200 and 700 degrees centigrade, shattered, buried or carried away every object in its path. This event, reporters said, was the culmination of years of simmering, molten pressure inside the volcano that finally erupted into a horrific act of nature.[7]

In a sudden flash of self-awareness, I saw the similarity between this devastation and my own behavior early in my professional life.

Deep within, I had been undergoing a powerful struggle for leadership, my emotions simmering for years until they finally erupted in an angry, foolish act that could have set my career back decades.

During an especially stressful merger and acquisition session, when I was trying to get a particularly important point across, I became so frustrated and angry towards one of the participants that my temper erupted, and I threw a chair across the room.

Silence followed, with all eyes upon me. Everyone, myself included, was astonished by my actions. Although I had displayed my temper in other meetings, even I knew that this time I had gone too far.

How had I reached this point of sheer irrationality? Early in my career, I had learned to accept my orders (or leadership objectives) with an attitude of bravado, preening with the personal power and authority granted me from the executive leadership. Added to this attitude was my assumption that everyone in the business arena knew there would be times when things would become bloody, even at the risk of losing most, if not all, of their friends.

And there was another conflict. Although I considered myself a leader, I was told by higher-ups exactly when and where I would be permitted to fight my organizational battles. Later, I realized that my sense of frustration and powerlessness to choose my battles could have been the seed that finally led to my destructive and irrational conduct that day in the boardroom.

My intent here is to share with you how my negative behavior as a leader and the shocking way I found myself communicating with others nearly destroyed my relations with executive management. With the ultimate irrational act of throwing that chair, I came close to losing everything I had worked for to promote my leadership career.

After this "incident," I found myself recalling seemingly insignificant warning signs pointing toward emotional upheaval and irrational behavior. These rumblings paralleled the minor eruptions of smoke and cinders that forewarned the world of the coming Mount St. Helens explosion. It seemed that regardless of the tasks I had to perform, or my skills, abilities or leadership development training, I was allowing my emotions to get in the way of my effectiveness as an acquisitions leader.

The simple fact is that, in the ideal world, leaders would react to input from other leaders (executives) and from followers (our employees) with perfect objectivity. But, as imperfect leaders, we filter and process experiences by returning to our ingrained values and beliefs.

This is why I needed to figure out what was going on within me, and learn how to identify those irrational beliefs, past experiences, or values that were creating unhealthy emotions and potentially sabotaging my leadership. I knew that I needed to replace these beliefs with healthier and more effective leadership choices.

I also needed to find what some emotional intelligence researchers term, "emotional depth and literacy." Simply stated, leaders must first understand what emotional intelligence *is* (emotional literacy), then become skilled at utilizing their emotions in the right way and at the right time (emotional depth).[8]

Unfortunately, my previous leadership models had led me to believe that good leaders create pain! This followed from the challenges that we as leaders toss out to our followers and our organizations. Supposedly, good leaders know this and are prepared to mop up the emotional messes we create. I realized that I needed to incorporate new communications skills to deal with the fallout from my actions.

Clearly, an attitude adjustment was a high priority. I could no longer afford to be a stranger to myself if, as a leader, I had to recognize how to emotionally respond to others in positive ways. Some of my past experiences, values, and personal beliefs were creating serious emotional blocks that began to fester into real productivity issues.

These blocks existed, not just for me as a leader, but also affected those I led in our quest to achieve mutual business goals. In other words, these blocks were creating self-defeating behavior patterns leading to high stress, reduced leadership effectiveness, and a lack of personal satisfaction at work for myself and my followers.

I learned that when I was leading others and a split between us arose over work-related tasks, serious tensions or conflicts emerged that diminished our productivity. In addition, my superiors found my actions to be particularly awkward. No surprise, right?

Soon, I was exhibiting career-limiting leadership behaviors such as winning at all costs, displaying anger, demeaning others, and retaliation. Executive coaches often call these acts *career stallers*.[8] Such behaviors represent negative personal attributes that, if left unchecked, can derail both one's leadership and one's livelihood.

For me, the prelude to change was introspection. I kept asking myself, "How did this happen?" I recognized that none of these attitudes had arisen overnight. My problems weren't simply fallout from the stressful experiences of handling multimillion-dollar mergers and acquisitions, restructuring business units or functions, reengineering work processes, or other special projects.

Instead, my arrogance had begun with a sense of cockiness from past successes. This attitude had developed into a self-delusion that I could do no wrong and that, as a leader, I was the greatest gift to my company since Jack Welch.

I realized that I had become so narcissistic as a leader that I considered myself invincible when it came to taking on assignments, roles, and responsibilities within the organization. Why wouldn't I believe my own press clippings? I was immortal!

In all fairness, some of my attitude derived from a history of acknowledgements, recognition, and praise from the executive team for years of successful acquisition negotiations. However, what I didn't realize until it was almost too late was that all of this background was actually making me a very ineffective leader.

Pride was, indeed, going before a fall. That realization was a turning point for me.

Ironically, perhaps the biggest problem I had was admitting that I had a leadership problem. I suspect that's the way it is with most people. I needed to find out why my staff was becoming so resistant to my direction because, at this point, it was almost impossible for me to be an effective leader and accomplish my assigned organizational goals and objectives.

Suddenly, from a leadership perspective, I was very lonely in the trenches with few, if any, followers. Others no longer felt confidence or trust in me. And what do you call a leader with no followers? Just another person taking a walk by himself.

I realized that I had to take specific steps to re-establish myself as the leader everyone wanted me to be. I needed to:

- Clarify the relationship between the message I thought I was communicating, and what I was actually communicating to my employees.

- Observe how my followers were filtering my words and language through their past experiences and values. Then, see how they ended up feeling about what I was communicating.

These steps may sound like simple practices, but how many of us know of colleagues or bosses around us in the workplace who just can't seem to master these behaviors?

As for myself, I gradually became aware that I had begun statements with words reflecting an absolutist philosophy that took the form of dogmatic "must's," "should's," "have to's," and "got to's." This unconscious habit elicited highly negative and destructive emotional responses from those around me.

In truth, I was a "rigid communicator," constantly setting up a natural rebuttal from my listeners and creating an "either you do this, or else" workplace environment, with no flexibility. Their response, of course, was the same as my communication—rigid, creating an "either, or else" workplace environment for me, too.

The bottom line was, I had to make sure I did not repeat the inappropriate behavior that resulted in negative consequences, such as throwing the chair.

Another insight I had was recognizing my need to be perfectly competent at every task. No leader will ever know everything there is to know about everything. So, if I believed I needed to be a leader with the wisdom of Solomon, I was setting myself up for failure.

I also needed to eliminate the belief that I had the right to depend on my staff to pull me through each project while I led the charge. In fact, I had even thought that if things didn't go (or stay) the way I wanted them to, it would be catastrophic!

I was now determined to transform these irrational beliefs into a new, more effective and enlightened understanding about my leadership. I strove to communicate more positively, saying, "I would like," or "it is my desire that," or "it is my hope that" we are capable or strong enough to make each acquisition a success.

If I were to take a moment to reflect on lessons I learned from my chair-throwing incident, I would say that I needed to begin changing the way I communicated with my staff. I had to change my philosophy from an absolutist approach to one that was more flexible in communication and expectations, creating reasonable objectives.

Open, coherent and non-threatening channels of communication are essential to eliminate the "must's," "should's," and "have to's" I had so thoughtlessly used during acquisitions. In business today, we need to replace such negative reinforcement with a greater sense of cooperation and collaboration.

For me, this recognition was the beginning of developing an emotional intelligence that has paid dividends many times over throughout my career. I found new satisfaction in leading others by inspiring them, and I discovered that learning to speak the language of inspiration is vital for success in all truly effective leadership moments.

In addition, I learned that a real leader can change his or her approach to leadership and become more agile and adaptive. As I began to consciously practice this new outlook, my career quickly accelerated. In fact, I began to build my entire vocational future around it. I eventually became a managing partner for a firm that creates human resources systems, and then a Vice President of Human Resources for a global enterprise.

I believe that two of the most common leadership problems in organizations today are performance anxiety (fueled by fear of losing our jobs) and emotional outbursts or anger towards management, employees, or co-workers. While it is important to acknowledge having these feelings, we must not do so in such a way that they will interfere with our value as individuals and efficacy as leaders.

Rather, if we are to achieve the kind of sustainable futures we all desire in our organizations, we must learn to master the art of engaging in critical conversations with constructive concern and positive empathy, or what many call *appreciative inquiry*.[10] The reward will be a workplace that's less confrontational and more conducive to increasing the productivity of those who must produce.

When tempted to unleash the ultra-intense clouds of volcanic emotions, I now channel my energies into expanding my abilities and those of others, practicing more positive behaviors based on rational, not irrational, beliefs.

Since that fateful day when I threw the chair across the room, I have learned that truly effective leadership demands that we develop strong character and the emotional maturity to communicate effectively. After all, what organization wants a potential Mount St. Helens in its leadership ranks?

4

Surviving in the Financial Services Jungle: Constancy Amid Chaos

John Lohre

On January 14, 2004, Bank One announced a merger with JPMorgan Chase, creating the second largest bank in the U.S. Though it was major news for the general public, the merger was probably no surprise for many pundits of the financial services industry. Since the late 1970's, increasing competition has fueled a frenzy of bank consolidations. A third of all banks have gradually disappeared— approximately 84% through mergers, the rest through operational failures.[11]

In many respects, at least part of the industry has become a "bank-eat-bank" jungle. Prior to merging with JPMorgan Chase, Bank One was well known for acquiring regional banks as a growth strategy. In fact, that's how I was introduced to Bank One—through a strategic merger.

At the time, I was a Vice President of Corporate Banking for a regional institution. We were the target of an unfriendly takeover by Marshall and Ilsley Bank. To fend off this attack, our executives went searching for another "white knight" to acquire us. Our savior was Bank One. Although Bank One had a strong retail presence that we sorely needed, I soon learned that merging with this behemoth was a mixed blessing. It had propelled us into a much larger culture replete with negative politics, interpersonal intrigue, and corporate bureaucracy.

My tenure at Bank One was a personal turning point in my career and in my leadership growth. I discovered that surviving the fire of chaotic circumstances requires tremendous inner resolve, level-headedness, and hope. It demands every ounce of endurance a person can muster.

To lead effectively, I had to reach deep into my soul to tap hidden reserves of optimism, fortitude, and integrity. In the process, I also learned that calm consistency can become invaluable in the "permanent whitewater"[12] of organizational change.

To me, achieving this ideal state meant exhibiting human decency, patience, and long-suffering in my leadership. Cultivating such inner constancy became a guiding compass, shaping my legacy at Bank One as I tried to stoically face organizational turbulence, upheaval, and change on a daily basis.

The Chaos Begins

By the time we merged with Bank One, I had worked at my $3 billion Milwaukee-based bank for 14 years. I had been hired right out of law school. Having grown up in Milwaukee, I cultivated my personal contacts as business opportunities for the bank. Distinguishing myself in commercial mortgages, I rose to Assistant General Counsel, and then to VP of Corporate Banking. In the process, I also befriended many executives with special banking needs, often referring them to our Private Banking team.

About a year after merging with Bank One, my success in sending clients to Private Banking paid off—my supervisor informed me that I had been recommended for a position as Assistant Manager in the Private Banking group. I was ecstatic. My ship had finally come in!

I had just turned 40 and saw this as an opportunity to provide broader leadership at the bank while catching a "golden ring on the merry-go-round of life." To say the least, the prospect of becoming an important player in a strong retail banking operation appealed to my ambitious side.

My transfer to Private Banking received all the hoopla of a promotion, but I didn't realize that it would also mark the beginning of a roller-coaster ride through a maze of broken promises, backstabbing, and betrayals.

The stack of disappointments quickly began to grow. My transfer's appeal had been partly due to a promise that I would replace a senior Private Banking officer named Norm. Norm was retiring, and I was to work with him for about six months and then take over his accounts.

As soon as I joined the group, however, Norm reneged on his retirement. Married to a woman 20 plus years his junior, he suddenly decided that he was in no hurry to retire until she did.

Norm's change of heart made my transition into Private Banking difficult. I had to "work my way" into his schedule just to meet his clients and join his meetings. I was also relegated to an office where few clients could find me, while Norm continued to enjoy his spacious room in a high-traffic area.

After months of watching others working busily away, I became somewhat depressed. I felt unneeded and unwanted, a "stray buoy in the sea of opportunity." I began pondering whether I should tough it out, rejoin my old Corporate Banking unit, or leave the bank altogether.

Realizing that frustration can drive people to desperate actions, I decided to keep my wits, keep the job, and try to redefine my leadership role in the department. At the time, I rationalized that my transfer had already been announced, senior managers were watching me, and I wanted to be loyal. Hoping that the annoyances would be temporary, I also wanted to prove I could be both a manager *and* a team player.

In retrospect, had I known what would transpire over the next four years, I might have taken the first exit out of the building to pursue a new career elsewhere. Yet, my decision to stay brought valuable lessons. I learned that leadership is often a test of unwavering determination, dogged endurance, and patient stamina rather than talent, brilliance, or heroic bravado. Gradually, my tenacity also won over my colleagues, who displayed increasing trust in my leadership abilities.

Seizing the Day

Another attraction of Private Banking was the fact that, as an Assistant Manager, I would be mentored by our department head, Doug, a well-educated and successful manager. Yet, this hope began to fade as I worked in Norm's shadow for over a year. One day, however, Norm became ill and subsequently retired. This brought my career back into gear, and I was finally promoted to Assistant Manager.

At last, I could work closely with Doug, who tutored me as a friend and colleague. I learned of his strengths and faults, and he learned of mine. We complemented each other well. Doug's impetuousness and fast-acting style were balanced by my soft-hearted, even-keeled approach. Although my leadership style was different from his, Doug and I made a great team.

Our mutual respect blossomed, and the results showed. Over the next year, Private Banking added three new outlying offices and doubled its staff. Everything seemed to be on track, and I was headed toward becoming a major player at Bank One.

Then, just as I was growing comfortable, the rug was pulled from under me once again. When a Private Banking manager at a remote branch left for a better position, Doug immediately moved his office to the remote branch on an "interim basis"—just until he could hire a new branch manager, or so he said. I naively went along with it, thinking that I'd inherit Doug's plush corner office, assume day-to-day leadership, and meet more frequently with executives. What I didn't realize was that Doug's real motive for moving was because he was at odds with his boss.

In fact, Doug had actually decided to leave the bank. Moving to the branch allowed him the space to prepare inconspicuously. Within 90 days, he had received an offer for a better position as an executive at a regional bank in Minneapolis.

Doug's departure was the first time someone close to me had left management. I was sad and energized at the same time—sad because my friend and mentor was gone, but energized because I was now a leading candidate to head the group.

Although John, the Executive VP of Retail Banking, later told me that Doug had *not* advocated my promotion before leaving, I actually thought that it was John who lacked confidence in me. Despite his reservations, a couple of weeks later (and two years after my joining Private Banking), John promoted me to unit head.

The ancient Roman soldier, Horace, once said, "Seize the day, but put as little trust as you can in tomorrow." Although pleased with the promotion, perhaps I should have been bracing myself for the next bump in the road.

Into the Lion's Den

My first weeks as the Department Head were "management by fire" as I grappled with new procedures and processes. Bank One's executives were flexing their muscle to achieve better results and earnings, but it was taking a toll on new people like me.

As for my team, I felt as if I were driving a 17-horse hitch wagon in a circus parade. Everyone had great ideas on how to excel and grow, but they all wanted to do it differently. It was difficult to "tighten the reins" and get everyone into the same corral.

I also grappled with inter-departmental clashes. In traditional retail lending, the prevailing philosophy is one of structure and discipline. "If it doesn't fit in the box, we don't do the deal." However, this isn't how Private Bankers think. They deal outside of the box and have greater leeway to close difficult transactions with innovative pricing. While retail units depend on volume, Private Bankers rely on relationships.

Because the retail units were not aware of the benefits of this background, they often felt that my area received preferential treatment, which provoked animosity, jealousy, and petty politics.

As a result, Private Banking didn't get many referrals from retail. Referrals came through Corporate Banking instead, which depended on us to keep the owners of their business customers happy. We, on the other hand, depended heavily on other retail areas for operational support and product assistance. With retail mindsets aligned more with "transactional leadership" ("What will it do for me?") than "transformational leadership" ("How can I inspire others to achieve?"), I sensed that conflict lay ahead.

I was right. Our Private Banking unit had a separate teller station that was off-limits to "normal" (retail) customers, thereby allowing special clients to bypass long teller lines. But we only had one teller, and in the teller's absence, we requested backup from other retail branches, a favor not easily granted.

In fact, on two prior occasions, retail units refused our pleas for help, claiming that they, too, were short-staffed. In the end, I used Andrea, an administrative assistant, to work the Private Banking teller station.

My team resented the fact that other retail departments had taken advantage of our desperate need by withholding their resources. Those areas were well-staffed with under-used tellers who could have easily helped us out. In hindsight, my team also probably thought that my patient tolerance of this situation contributed to my failure to resolve it.

However, one day, I was returning from a meeting and saw Andrea, our administrative assistant, at the Private Banking teller window yet again. The retail pool had smugly denied us the use of backup tellers a *third* time. My blood boiled, and I decided that enough was enough. I ordered Andrea to close her window immediately and then put a sign on it that read, "Teller Closed, Use Front Lobby," something that had never been done before.

This seemingly small action turned into an important defining moment. I had taken a firm stand, and although Private Banking clients grumbled and groused about waiting in teller lines, I had finally earned the respect of my Private Banking team. Now, they saw me as their leader, not just their manager.

A ripple effect quickly ensued. Our own executives used Private Banking for their personal accounts, so it wasn't long before our

Executive VP became aware of the situation and ordered a permanent teller backup for Private Banking to be provided by the retail pool.

Indeed, what goes around comes around. Our challenging situation had finally received a long-awaited measure of redress. In the process, I emerged as a stronger leader and gained the trust of my entire Private Banking department.

Developing Constancy

Through my experiences at Bank One, I learned several valuable lessons. For example, I learned that leadership is all about operating on a higher moral plane when relating to the needs of others, not just managing the bottom line or forwarding one's career.

I also discovered that becoming a leader is a process, not an instant transformation. It requires focus, involves trial and error, and can test personal integrity to the max.

Finally, I learned that great leaders exude constancy and relentless steadfastness under pressure, creating an energy that raises others to higher levels of personal and professional performance. In particular, three forms of constancy became guiding beacons to me: (a) constancy of character, (b) constancy of caring, and (c) constancy of commitment.

1.   *Constancy of Character*

English author-poet William Channing once said: "The greatest man is he who chooses the right with invincible resolution, who resists the sorest temptations from within and without, who bears the heaviest burdens cheerfully, who is calmest in storms and most fearless under menace and frowns."[13]

To me, this constancy of character reflects an authenticity that creates *groundedness* in the midst of difficulties. Constancy of character is about balancing positive attributes while practicing leadership. In our team's interaction with other retail units, for instance, it became vital to find the right mix of patience and firmness when standing my ground.

Besides balancing principles and attitudes, it becomes equally important to find the *right* ones to follow. I remember that Bill, one of our senior officers, used to tell ethnic jokes in the office. Although his jokes were benign, our middle-aged receptionist was of the same ethnic background as that of his humor. One day, she marched into my office, closed the door, and announced that she was embarrassed and mortified by Bill's lack of sensitivity. She demanded that Bill be reprimanded for his vulgarity.

My dilemma was clear. How do you explain lack of sensitivity to a senior officer while keeping him focused on sales and service? I decided that the right approach was to be bold but not overbearing, to stand firm but stay even-tempered.

When I brought Bill into my office, rather than scold him, I cajoled him. I was direct without naming anyone in particular. Bill pouted, complained about tough working conditions to deflect the heat, and then went back to work. In a couple of days, he was his normal self, minus the ethnic jokes.

Our receptionist trusted me after that. Now, she felt safe to come to me with office problems I might otherwise miss. Colin Powell once said that the day your people stop coming to you with their problems is the day you have stopped leading them.[14]

At any rate, I felt as if I had found a golden mean that created constancy of character. I had exercised resolve, but did so in a spirit of calmness, raising my team's performance. I had exhibited consistency with my principles and moral decency while resisting temptations to make mountains out of molehills.

By staying grounded throughout the storms, my sense of constancy had grown and leadership was getting easier—or was it?

2.   *Constancy of Caring*

Being new, I probably spent too much time working on my annual budget, which caused my boss angst—but not because I was slow. While I was trying to do a thorough job, John was looking for his next promotion. It didn't matter what kind of budget I proposed, John would do it his way. He eventually made sweeping changes to my budget so that it was almost impossible for me to achieve my budgetary goals.

Yet, as Joel Barker said, leaders take people where they wouldn't otherwise go.[15] So, I rallied my team and made up a new budget. It didn't improve the dynamic between John and me. In fact, he became even more antagonistic.

One day, John summoned me and Lynn, one of my top employees, to his office. The topic of conversation was a construction loan. About 90% of the loan had been paid out, but only 50% of the work had been finished. The contractor had gone bankrupt, and subcontractors had yet to be paid. The client was blaming the bank (and Lynn) for the fiasco, but bad loans happen. Still, John reprimanded us strongly.

As Lynn and I left his office, she turned to me with tears in her eyes and asked, "Am I going to be fired?" I responded with a resounding "No!" But the damage was done. She'd been intimidated. I felt bad and vowed to stick up for my team in the future. The Latin phrase, *vox dei, vox populi,* says that leaders may be appointed, but power comes by the sustaining of followers. In other words, if you care for your team, they will always be behind you.

The rift between John and me widened even more, as I tried to care about my people's well-being. John only cared about looking good, moving up, and achieving status. A Harvard MBA, he was completely obsessed with his career. He had reprimanded Lynn and me not because this loan had defaulted, but because he didn't want to look foolish to superiors. Conversely, my only desire was for my team to look good and for me to do my best.

Perhaps this is why my mentor, Doug, left the company. He was all too familiar with the careerism and political games. I learned a valuable lesson from this hullabaloo. What leaders care about and how they consistently manifest it makes all the difference.

John was a perfect example of what *not* to care about. In a negative way, he inspired me to develop constancy in caring for others, helping my staff to succeed through my decisions and actions. I also resolved to take a different path than Doug's, one of commitment to my team's cohesion through thick or thin, rather than to retreat at the first sign of trouble.

3. Constancy of Commitment

Although I wanted to lead the Private Banking department into a series of changes for the better, things were about to get worse. After Doug took his new job in Minneapolis, he started recruiting my most talented staff. I felt powerless to stop him. One by one, they left for greener pastures.

The first to go was my Assistant Manager, Jean. Next was an administrative assistant, then an employee at an outlying branch. Finally, another VP and top sales officer left for a position at an insurance agency. While I supported her in this decision, somehow I had to stop the talent drain. Using Doug's strategy, I, too, began recruiting from other banks.

Beyond the staffing issues, my boss, John, confided in me once that he was uncomfortable talking to superiors about credit, his weakest area of knowledge. Personally, I suspect that this insecurity also fueled his paranoia, craving for control, and penchant for politics. To compensate, John created a loan committee, consisting of retail lenders, leasing agents, and indirect (car dealer) loan managers.

Private Banking didn't fit well within this mix, since our loans didn't fit within the box. The committee ended up chiding us for "off the wall" lending practices, which only deepened John's mistrust of my leadership.

The tension continued to increase when bank examiners found irregularities in our Private Banking loan portfolio. It didn't matter that the loans had been made before I joined the department. The examiners were "rattling their swords," and John worried about looking bad to his superiors.

One day, he called our entire team into his office and vehemently swore at us. When it was my turn to speak, I calmly asked everyone to come in on a weekend, go through the files, and correct the situation. When the examiners came back a month later, we passed just fine. Still, word spread that Private Banking "didn't know what they were doing."

My commitment to the company during all of this havoc never waned. My resolve to provide steady leadership intensified and bound our team together. In the words of Calvin Coolidge:

> *Nothing in this world can take the place of persistence. . . . Persistence and determination alone are omnipotent. The slogan "press on" has solved and always will solve the problems of the human race.*

I learned that true leadership demands commitment to a worthy cause and a staying power that inspires others with hope.

Betrayal and Taking the Higher Road

After working feverishly for about a year, things finally started to come together. I had rebuilt my team, was making my budget, and had fixed broken processes. I had even earned some respect from other retail areas. I felt upbeat and positive, but my optimism would be severely tested. The day before our monthly department meeting, John came down to my office, closed the door, and sat down in an over-stuffed chair across from my desk. I wasn't sure what was on his mind, but I felt that since things were going so well, it was probably good news. I smiled and gave him my full attention.

John cleared his throat and said, "Due to many reasons, I am replacing you as Head of Private Banking immediately."

I was dumbstruck. "What things, John? What have I done wrong?"

John mumbled, "People leaving, and other things." I pressed him for more information, but he wouldn't elaborate. He said, "I am going on vacation. When I get back, we'll get together and discuss the reasons. For now, I want you to meet with your successor tonight, after hours, to go over her transition into your office."

"What will happen to me? Am I fired?" I asked, shaken.

"No," John reassured me. "You have a place here. I would like you to stay on to help with the transition."

Angry, confused, and deeply hurt, it took all my energy to keep my wits. "Do the President and CEO know what's happening?" I asked through gritted teeth.

"Yes," John replied.

"And what did they say?" I asked intently.

"They told me not to lose you; to try and keep you here."

When John left, I immediately called my friend, Mike, a senior VP at the bank. Mike was astounded, but there was nothing he could do. Determined to figure it out, I asked the Head of Human Resources for my personnel records, but found nothing unusual.

When I arrived home, I informed my wife of the day's events and proceeded to have a sleepless night. I knew that I didn't want to go quietly into the sunset. I felt that I had been wronged and was ready to walk into the President's office and . . . do what? I needed to calm down and think.

I decided to meet with my successor, Anne, who acted with grace and charm, knowing that it would be difficult for both of us. She was positive and wanted to work together; yet, she was cut from the same cloth as John, with little lending experience and a big retail bias (exactly what Private Banking *didn't* need).

Still, she was careful not to malign me, the outgoing leader. Anne needed me on her side. I wondered if I should play along with the charade or upset the order of things by causing a stir. I opted for leading by example in staying the course. I wanted my team to have continuity. Anne was a good process manager but not a people leader. I could help in that arena.

The next day, as everyone gathered for our monthly meeting, John announced that I had helped Private Banking through a difficult time, thanked me, and named Anne as the new Head. Seeing the shocked expressions on everyone's faces pained me deeply. It was the worst moment of my banking career.

Yet, I had to stand tall and be a leader. I knew that everyone was looking to me, and I needed to be there for them. Without waiting for John's invitation, I spontaneously assured the team that I was staying to make the transition easier for Anne. I could see the relief on John's and Anne's faces.

As I went back to my office for the last time, much to my surprise,

I wasn't alone. The entire Private Banking department walked into my room, closed the door, and began wringing their hands, crying and grumbling about injustice.

Although I appreciated their loyalty, I stopped their comments cold and told them not to dislike their new manager before they got to know her. I urged them to work toward unification, not dissolution. After some hugs and handshakes, everyone went back to work, leaving me to myself.

Life Beyond Bank One

Two weeks later, John returned from vacation and stopped by my (now smaller) office. He said he owed me that talk about his reasons for the change. I told him it was not necessary, knowing that our discussion would only be superficial, anyway. I recognized that life is too short to keep a grudge.

Besides, my friends at the bank were already looking for new positions for me in their departments. Anne and I continued to "co-manage" for almost a year. She was a good soldier for John. We disagreed at times about direction, but never in front of the team. It was stressful, but I remained true to my convictions and values—it was all I could do.

Through my contacts within the bank, eventually I landed a position in Trust and Investments. One of my former mentors had been promoted to Head of Personal Trust five years earlier. Anne was probably relieved to see me go, while John received his promotion to President of Bank One's Fort Worth office at about the same time.

One day, I noticed an article in the newspaper about a new private bank that was coming to Milwaukee. I recognized the CEO and wrote him a congratulatory letter. He called me a couple of days later and asked if I would consider an interview to become the bank's

President. I accepted the invitation, but we both knew the selection process had already been well under way.

Still, the CEO was impressed with my credentials and said that he would call when he was ready to provide trust and investments. I thanked him for his time and thought nothing more of it. Two years later, however, the CEO was true to his word. I received a call from him, left Bank One, and never looked back.

In the midst of disorder, deceitfulness, and deviousness, I had done my level best to perform at Bank One. I learned that if you treat your staff the same way you would want to be treated, you can always lead without regrets. Also, if you avoid placing yourself above your staff, your team will always make your position "priority one."

The strongest leaders don't vacillate or compromise when it comes to principles like these; rather, they remain true and constant to their ideals, regardless of the threats or consequences.

Victor Frankl said, "Everything can be taken from a person but one thing: the last of human freedoms . . . to choose one's attitude in any given set of circumstances."[16]

I was confident that I had chosen wisely. Although I was sidelined in my career, blindsided by my boss, and broadsided by political infighting, I was never sidetracked from my ethical values and integrity.

Reflecting on my career, I am grateful for the gift of constancy that I cultivated in the crucible of adversity. Today I am the father of four grown children. I've learned that one's personal life demands just as much constancy as does business. In fact, it presents just as much turmoil, if not more!

Now, my children bring me their own leadership problems and ask for my advice and counsel. As tough as my lessons were at Bank One, they have helped me greatly in this regard.

I believe it behooves each of us who has been or will be blessed to serve in influential positions now or in the future to provide steady, unwavering leadership, the kind that imbues moral courage, adherence to sound principles, constancy, and hope. This chaotic world certainly needs it, and if we don't provide it, who will?

5

Unveiling the Leader Within: The Power of Intentional Leadership

Peter Amato

At the tender age of 37, I was jolted awake one day to discover that, not only hadn't I been truly alive, but I was slowly dying. At the time, I was the sole inhabitant of a tiny, self-centered, self-seeking world. Yet, oddly enough, I was totally empty. What a paradox!

My journey began in 1955, when I was born the fourth child of a hard-working, lower-middle-class Italian father and a loving Polish mother, parents who—driven and proud—struggled to grind out their version of the American Dream. My dad started an automotive parts and accessories business the year I was born, and the family business soon became the center of his world and our own.

By age thirteen, I had joined my two older brothers and my sister in supporting the business; in fact, in all my years living at home, the only thing I remember ever being discussed was "the business." As a teenager, I worked seven days a week after school and on weekends. When my father became ill, my oldest brother, Joseph, became the patriarch of the business, sacrificing his education to keep the store open. My brother, Dennis, joined next, then my sister, Barbara, and then finally, myself.

My father was a blend of tremendous business savvy and a warm heart. He dreamed of sending me to college so that I could become an educated contributor toward a greater future for our prospective "big business."

His dream would, in fact, come true in every detail. His small business grew to 25 retail stores and a one-million-square-foot wholesale division, including the worldwide import/export of our products, as well as the development of a private brand of products. In time, we employed over 1,000 people and became the largest business of our type in the world.

I, as it turned out, would receive an education far beyond the walls of academia.

As I grew up, my career in the family business of distributing automotive parts globally—both wholesale and retail—evolved from mopping floors and cleaning glass cases to retail sales, warehouse work, phone sales, road sales, purchasing, marketing, advertising, and finally, to business administration.

As the business thrived, I began to explore, with great enthusiasm, the material realms of success. I loved high-performance automobiles, and had a passion for motor sports that equaled my devotion to ensuring our family's livelihood.

I began drag racing professionally and collecting exotic sports cars, such as Porsches, Mercedes-Benz, Ferraris, and Lamborghinis. My hero was my oldest brother, Joseph, who went on to eventually become a five-time world champion in NHRA drag racing and was recognized for some time as having won the most championships in the history of the sport.

As the business expanded worldwide, we had our private jet in the hangar and two full-time pilots on standby. I wore ten-thousand-dollar, custom-made suits and handmade shoes, which told me that I was powerful, proud, and enjoying the fruits of success and good fortune.

But in time, my life became a terrible mess. I was all shiny on the outside, but I felt desperate and hopeless on the inside. I was beginning to realize that material success was not enough to sustain any form of happiness or wholeness. As the days and weeks went by, I grew painfully aware that something was missing.

Like many others whose lives are spiritually and emotionally empty, I began drinking daily. Drug use followed, especially when I wanted to celebrate my achievements. Soon, I became a slave to drugs and alcohol. My skin became jaundiced and I pushed everyone away while I isolated myself with my drug of choice at that time.

Visine and handkerchiefs became my best friends, and I pretended that I had a head cold—for twenty years! Alternating between feeling homicidal and suicidal, I could hardly believe where life had taken me. In my new world of seclusion and paranoia intensified by drug abuse, I was now constantly alone, and very afraid.

My marriage to my high-school sweetheart was suffering badly, and to escape from the tension, I began doing the afternoon and evening bar circuit. As my drinking progressed, I spiraled down even farther, losing touch with reality and finding myself in dingy bars I once would have shunned. At some level, I recognized that I actually fit in and belonged in these places. In fact, they began to feel like home.

As I steadily plummeted toward rock bottom, I often experienced blackouts, later to awake and find deep scars not only on my body but within my soul. And this would have continued, probably leading to my death—or that of someone else—were it not for a local judge who had been observing my steady decline.

One day, he called my family and handed down his ultimatum: either I entered a rehabilitation facility, or I would go straight to jail. For once, I made the right decision: I choose rehab. That was the beginning of my journey toward personal mastery and self-leadership, or what I call, *Intentional Leadership.*

When I entered the facility, I found myself in the midst of seventy-four other drug and alcohol addicts from every walk of life. A few days after I began detoxification, I realized that I wasn't in rehab to please the judge: I was there to save my life. There is nothing like withdrawal from addictive substances to reveal the layers of packaging, false beliefs, and warped perceptions that have slowly encased oneself. I had become a prisoner, wrapped in invisible chains that had become almost unbreakable.

Now, as they began falling away, I became aware that Ferraris, private jets, and power were not the gifts I had received by being a business leader; they were merely props that helped to sustain my false sense of ego or self-importance. They, along with my addictions, had masked the gnawing void of meaninglessness inside me.

In rehab, I discovered that this inner dissonance had opened the doorway to my drug abuse and alcoholism, a potentially fatal disease. I gradually realized that I was not invincible, as I had once believed. And for the very first time in my life, I saw the promise of surrendering to a Higher Power, truly discovering who I really was, and finding peace within.

Today, I understand that my addiction was really a misdirected search for spirituality. My therapists showed me that I was removed not only from my community, but from my very essence and spirit. The only way out was to reconnect with my spiritual self and to look inward—to rediscover that scintillating ambience of my inner core, the true me.

As I slowly regained my physical health, I began the daily practice of meditation. A friend in recovery told me that I could discover who I really was by sitting still, focusing inward, and centering attention on my breathing. As I did, I began to recognize the difference between my *self image* (what I believed I was) and my *true self.* In time, meditation became my path back to sanity and humility. It helped me remember who I was, and in so doing, achieve a peace that really does surpass all understanding. It also led to my belief that successful leaders learn to strip away ego, leading from more spiritually-grounded values.

When I re-entered the normal world, I found myself filled with a desire to serve others in a variety of ways and a variety of places: locally, regionally, and internationally. I think this is when my inner sense of servant leadership began to really blossom. I strove to become a voice to help create change and eliminate human suffering—a far cry from my previous orientation to please only myself in every way possible.

As my volunteer work and personal search to reconnect with my true self proceeded, I eventually learned that I could best love myself by loving others. Only then did I realize that we are all interconnected, and that love is at the heart of true leadership.

I now recognized a much higher calling in life than collecting money, possessions, and achievements. I was overflowing with a newfound inner sense of spirituality that I had previously suppressed. I thirsted to understand it and began to study, teach, and travel in the name of spirituality. I just couldn't absorb enough of it.

It became clear that this new "me" was being guided from within; therefore, I began to nurture myself as a whole person, meditating daily, choosing a healthy diet, and taking nutritional supplements combined with regular massages and daily walking. Every day, I felt a stronger alignment and sense of oneness with my inner spirituality, and I liked the feeling!

Following my new dream to be an agent of positive change, I studied with many renowned spiritual leaders. I was also led to the jungles of Africa to experience more of nature's healing power. Kalahari Bushmen, wise men, and indigenous healers all touched my life, and I came to realize that most of us only use a tiny percent of our innate capacities. These experiences stretched my ability to see and feel beyond the norm and to develop the leadership direction that would transform my life forever.

It has now been over 13 years since I chose the path of light versus darkness. I have studied world religions, wisdom traditions, and spiritual philosophies across the globe, learning that it is vital to connect with each other at this pivotal juncture of history.

Rather than remaining solitary and fearful of engaging with our fellow human beings, I believe our survival actually depends on our ability to cultivate unity and reciprocal generosity.

As an expression of my new sense of direction, I began performing pioneering work in the field of integrative medicine, which treats the whole person in mind, body, and spirit. This practice integrates age-old healing arts with modern medicine, spiritual growth, and emotional freedom. When I co-founded the National Integrative Medicine Council with Dr. Andrew Weil and accepted the position as chairman of the board, I expressed a desire to influence change within health care, politics, and religion.

I initially focused exclusively on health care reform, but over time I have realized that people resist change due to patterned conditioning. In order to embrace change, we must first open ourselves to higher forms of learning. This has become the foundation of my personal leadership philosophy.

I believe that leadership is about creating a new story, tapping into a fresh outlook, and enhancing one's condition by opening up to higher forms of learning. At the same time, it is important to be patient, both with ourselves and with others.

This awareness has launched me into the latest phase of my journey as a social leader, which has exceeded my wildest dreams. I teach workshops and speak to those in the healthcare field, in corporations, in prisons, and in drug courts. I also work with adolescents facing personal challenges.

I like to call this approach *Intentional Leadership* because the center of my work is to reveal the whole person, to free people from past modes of limiting beliefs and behaviors, and to find truth at a deeper level of reality. This is our profound challenge as leaders in every aspect of life and organizations.

In this sense, Intentional Leadership becomes a prelude to other leadership models, such as servant leadership. Intentional Leadership requires a leader not only to honor the truth of mankind's diversity, but also to underscore the uniqueness of the inner individual.

Intentional Leadership gives rise to a sense of connectedness once we begin to understand our divine natures. Servant leaders put this understanding to work through collaboration, service, and an authentic "being in the world" (or *dasein* as philosopher Martin Heidegger called it).[17]

Often, people may realize that our manner of existence is broken, but they cannot see that they are broken, as well. We are the cause as well the effect. Once we realize this, we can move forward towards approaching life in a fresher, healthier way. That's Intentional Leadership at work.

When I became sober, I realized that the root cause of my addiction was a "soul disconnect." This awareness became living water that nourished me on my journey toward inner harmony. Now, when I notice sadness and frustration in others around me, I try to assist by showing that we are each capable of developing Intentional Leadership: the power to change ourselves and our destinies from within.

I have found that we are all born with natural capacities to lead, and can cultivate our leadership insights by listening to our intuition and tapping into our divine potential. By pursuing a sense of purpose and inner harmony, thus transforming our own lives, we can become catalysts in enhancing life for everyone else around us. I know—I've embraced the process and have tasted its fruits.

Today, I am writing a book and designing a curriculum of personal growth that will teach children, recovering addicts, and employees in the workplace how to become Intentional Leaders. Thanks to a grant by the Department of Education, we are beginning to teach meditation to children in selected public schools. My hope is that this small step will lead to greater growth and change for millions of people over time.

Through my personal turning point—my recovery from rock bottom and realization of my life's mission—I have discovered that each of us has a mind, body, and spirit that exude innate greatness. Each of us can become a leader as we develop intentionality by nurturing our whole selves and our inner sense of meaning. In this way, we can overcome the challenges that arise within us and around us, whether at home, at the office, within our families, or in life.

And only through the quiet achievement of true inner balance and harmony can we each unleash the power of positive change, a change born of introspective intentionality that ultimately unveils the leader within.

6

Practicing Spirit-centered Leadership: Lessons from a Corporate Layoff

Arthur L. Jue

Turning and turning in the widening gyre
The falcon cannot hear the falconer;
Things fall apart; the centre cannot hold;
Mere anarchy is loosed upon the world,
The blood-dimmed tide is loosed, and everywhere
The ceremony of innocence is drowned;
The best lack all convictions, while the worst
Are full of passionate intensity.
(W. B. Yeats, The Second Coming)[18]

On the day that my professional life would turn upside down, I was sitting in my office, staring at my computer screen and trying to concentrate. Yet, despite my best intentions, I felt distracted and uneasy. For weeks, quietly whispered rumors of "significant changes" had been circulating around the company, feeding the fears of my office mates and creating an atmosphere of tension and impending doom.

A relatively new employee, I'd been brought aboard the good ship IBM as an entry-level mainframe programmer, despite having had none of the usual prerequisite coursework in college. Actually, my manager had told me early on that he had hired me not for my computer skills, but for my "leadership potential." I was flattered, grateful, and determined to learn my duties and perform at my level best.

The Chaos Begins

On this fateful day, quietly immersed in the cerebral world of bits and bytes, I allowed myself to be lulled by the surface appearances of normalcy—the day seemed like any other, intellectually rigorous but emotionally uneventful.

Suddenly, loud shouts erupted in the hallway and frightened, panicky cries filled the air. Office workers stampeded through the hallways, and my office mate and I sat frozen to our chairs, wondering what on earth was happening.

Then, quite unexpectedly, one of my co-workers burst through the doorway into my office and gasped, "We may never see each other again, but I couldn't let them take me away before I said good-bye!"

Breathless as he leaned against the wall, my friend—let's call him Norm—had just escaped what appeared to be armed guards who were attempting to haul him off like a common criminal. His destination: a temporary holding area that some of us would later call the "containment room."

As hastily as he had entered and without waiting for a response, Norm dashed off again, sprinting down the hallway and repeating the same urgent, heartrending farewell to other colleagues as frazzled security guards chased him in hot pursuit. My colleague and I sat speechless, looking at each other with eyes wide and mouths agape while the stark realization of what was happening gradually dawned on us.

Apparently, a firing blitz had begun, but hardly a humane one. With terrified employees darting around the building seeking support from their peers, and trying to elude the heavies who were assigned to escort them out, mayhem was breaking loose.

Both my office mate and I were new hires, and we reasoned that we, too, would become victims of this newly launched internal madness. I, in particular, had such limited programming experience that I felt certain I was destined for the containment room in the next few minutes.

We anxiously awaited the arrival of security guards to haul us away, but luckily (or so we thought at the time) both of us were spared the fate of Norm and many of our colleagues. Meanwhile, others were subjected to a travesty of professional behavior that led to traumatic, life-altering calamities for thousands of IBM families.

That dark time in the early 1990's marked a defining moment for the IBM Corporation and for many of its employees, including me. The massive layoff had commenced as part of a grand downsizing strategy, the first in IBM's history, but sadly not the last.

In time, I would witness many future downsizings during my years at IBM, and even be responsible for planning some of them as a manager. Still, these harsh images of this first layoff would remain indelibly engraved in my memory as a reminder of what can happen when an organization's leadership falters and its culture begins to deteriorate.

Leadership in Decline

For years, IBM had been an unequaled powerhouse in the information technology industry and highly regarded throughout the world as a paragon of organizational greatness. The company's close-knit culture had been universally envied and emulated by a plethora of aspiring enterprises. In fact, IBM's policy of lifelong employment had become legendary.[19]

Due in part to paternalistic-style management philosophies, errors by employees were commonly regarded as management's failure to provide appropriate leadership. Managers tended to perceive their roles as patriarchal, pursuing success by ensuring that all employees rowed in the same direction, like automatons or *cogs-in-the-wheel*.[20] This assumption was perpetuated through the indoctrination of managers and employees in IBM's leadership development and training programs.[21]

IBM's founder, Thomas J. Watson, also believed that re-training employees was preferable to termination. During the Great Depression, for example, rather than lay off the workforce, Watson preferred to retain and even hire more employees. He kept them busy over-producing and stashing away unsold inventory in preparation for an economic recovery.[22]

According to lore, when a junior executive made an error that cost the company 10 million dollars in losses, the man was summoned to Watson's office. The young man said, "I guess you want my resignation," whereupon Watson responded, "You can't be serious. We've just spent $10 million educating you!"[23]

As a result of Watson's ethic, terminations in IBM were historically well below industry averages. High morale, optimism, and even arrogance ensued as traditions created a culture of unparalleled cohesion and trust by employees towards management.[24]

As a new hire, I was enamored of these legends, and I readily embraced the company's socialization processes. Heroic tales about IBM's leadership had resulted in similar esprit de corps among the firm's more than 370,000 workers at the time. The formalization and publication of IBM's Basic Beliefs, a creed that espoused "respect for the individual,"[25] also reinforced a strong sense of group identity through collective trust in the system—this was "the IBM Way."

However, although this framework of company values was initially one of its greatest strengths, IBM's culture gradually sank into tragic weakness. The company's paternalistic management philosophy began to breed a subtle dependency and complacency among many employees. Job security became an entitlement, and "the boss always knew best."

In the late 1980's, visible signs of poor marketplace results finally revealed to the world that IBM had entered troubled waters.

As IBM's performance suffered, internal conflicts increased, and the disparity between the company's operational strategy and marketplace realities widened.[26] Age-old espoused values seemed to become unsustainable financially, and something had to give.

Still, news of IBM's first layoffs not only shocked the world but also destroyed long-held myths regarding Big Blue's invincibility. IBM's culturally inconsistent, drastic, and almost hysterical actions during the layoff probably helped fuel some of the early entrepreneurial fervor that ensued during the dot-com boom in Silicon Valley and elsewhere.

For example, after the first layoff, many of my peers took second jobs "just in case." Several friends fled to dot-coms, and one of my colleagues even enrolled in police academy training. I later spotted him at our local Taco Bell restaurant where he was moonlighting as a security guard.

The Human Spirit: Too High a Casualty

Beyond the financial and economic losses, IBM's initial round of layoffs psychologically devastated the victims' families and drastically altered their quality of life. In some respects, I have first-hand experience in this regard because when I hired into the company, I became a "second-generation" IBM'er. My father had worked at the company for nearly 30 years. When hired in the early 1960's, he was among the first Asian-Americans to enter IBM's workforce and contributed much to the company's success, enjoying IBM's rise to greatness.

Although my father rarely speaks of the nightmare surrounding IBM's first layoffs, I know that he was deeply affected. With sadness, he witnessed many of his friends struggling to survive the shock of losing their jobs. Some terminated employees had no clue how to prepare a resume, prospect for jobs, or undergo a job interview.

Though my father was spared during the initial draconian layoffs, he eventually opted for early retirement, which occurred much sooner than our family had anticipated. Somehow, the disillusionment with corporate duplicity had finally gotten the best of numerous employees from my father's generation, perhaps including himself.

Judi Neal, Executive Director of the *Center for Spirit at Work*, noted that firms have traditionally focused on "materialism and money, not people—a dark, heavy energy. There are people who just can't handle that anymore. They don't want to live in such a dispirited way . . . . They leave."[27]

After the immediate frenzy of the layoffs subsided, I watched employees wandering empty halls in search of survivors. At times, the scene resembled the aftermath of a war zone. Some employees scrounged vacant offices for memorabilia by which to remember friends who had been laid-off. Our managers appeared haggard and worn. They seemed to have aged a thousand years in a single day. Those of us who were left behind to "take up the slack" watched the evening news closely. Local media clips revealed post-layoff repercussions daily.

I recall news reports of an employee who smashed his car into a company office building, hurling a smoke bomb into the lobby. The garage of an executive's home was gutted in a fire started by a suspected arsonist. There was talk of one despondent employee who jumped off the roof of an IBM manufacturing facility. Suicide attempts, vandalism, litigation, and unionizing efforts seemed to proliferate as ominous clouds of uncertainty descended on the company.

Back at the office, survivors worried and wondered. Would Big Blue last? Would it break into Baby Blues? Could the company recover its lost marketplace position?

The public may never discover just how close IBM came to the edge of the abyss (possible bankruptcy) as leaders floundered to salvage it through restructuring efforts. Yet, evidences of a terrible tear in the fabric of human spirit seemed to abound as the company's leadership unraveled at the seams.

Invoking Spirit-centered Leadership

At the time of IBM's initial layoffs, my first reaction was to mind my own business, naively considering myself fortunate to keep clicking away on my company-owned computer yet another day. But deep inside, I wanted to hide from the ever-present reminders of the pain, hurt, and betrayal that had decimated the lives of my colleagues. Caught between the two responses to the firings, I struggled with the gnawing question: How *should* I respond? Should I retreat emotionally, or should I try to find, within my limited sphere of influence, some way that I could help?

From such inner questioning emerged an idea that I've since coined as *spirit-centered leadership*, the ability of anyone, whether traditionally religious or not, to demonstrate the spiritual principles of faith, love, and service that contribute to strong leadership. To be a spirit-centered leader one need only convey one's connection with "spirit"—the powerful universal force that permeates everything and enlivens everyone.

Spirit-centered leaders can exist anywhere, whether in a synagogue or in city hall. Spirit-centered leadership can even become manifested in a war zone, perhaps not unlike IBM's during its first layoff.

Spirit-centered leadership can be most valuable in coping with the increasing turmoil, challenges, and complexity confronting most organizations. Although this characterization may be a gross over-simplification of an intricate topic (my doctoral dissertation on the subject was 700 pages), I believe spirit-centered leadership represents an organizational imperative for the 21st Century.[28]

My experiences at IBM and elsewhere have confirmed my conviction of this fact. Though I did not realize it back then, IBM's harrowing first layoffs were a defining moment in shaping my leadership philosophy and attitudes, particularly toward employee-employer relations in the corporate milieu. They stimulated intense introspection, causing me to adopt many principles of spirit-centered leadership in coping with the effects of corporate brutalism and "organizational domination."[29]

Putting Principles into Practice

For me, lessons in spirit-centered leadership gradually unfolded through opportunities to help revitalize the company's spirit. I began to better understand how leaders become more effective as they reflect their spiritual principles in their behavior, replacing selfishness with supportiveness, "doing" with "being," and fear with faith. And always striving to place people before programs!

Of course, numerous principles of spirit-centered leadership exist, but I will focus on only three here: (a) being versus doing; (b) faith versus fear; and finally, (c) people versus programs.

1.   *"Being" versus "Doing"*

Western management typically favors external action over reflection and analysis. We are taught at an early age that the squeaky wheel gets the grease. In business, we coerce, build, master, win, compete, motivate, perform—all action words. The assumption is that we operate in an economic meritocracy based on developing competence and skills. Firms generally succeed based on the value of what they can deliver, versus what they collectively represent. Always, the emphasis is on *active doing*.

Conversely, other traditions reflect a "less is more" aesthetic. For example, in the Japanese martial art of Aikido and minimalist trends in the fine arts, practitioners generate meaningful outcomes through non-action, rather than action. Stillness becomes powerful as small, simple strokes can produce profound results.[30]

On the day of IBM's first layoffs, I recall discussing with my parents how I should react. I was numb. I couldn't eat. I wept as I recounted what had happened to my friend Norm earlier that morning. I expressed my concerns about the future of my company, my peers, and myself. Should I quit, join unionizing efforts, work longer, try harder, disengage, or take a different path?

Wisely, my mother counseled me to step back from the fray, see the big picture, and simply *be* my best self. With that straightforward statement, she magically changed my focus from competence to character, from doing to being. She helped me to see when less is more.

Harvard professors, Ronald Heifitz and Martin Linsky, compare this process to a metaphor of *stepping away from the dance floor to observe the dance*.[31] That is, in the crisis of a leadership moment, they encourage leaders to become meditative or self-reflective *before* acting.

My parents encouraged me not to react to the effects of the layoffs as a victim, but instead to alter my frame of reference so I could view IBM from a different lens. They suggested that I consider myself a company owner, rather than an employee.

Adopting this "being" mode, rather than entering a "doing" mode, eventually helped me behave much differently than I probably would have otherwise. It helped me to develop an inner peace and stillness amid the turmoil and chaos around me, and I began to focus on my character, rather than on external events. My new demeanor was hardly dramatic, but nonetheless yielded powerful interpersonal results.

As I opted to become reflective, I better understood that although I could not change the past, I could make choices in the present that would affect my future. I could actually choose to be sad or happy, dispirited or renewed, frazzled or contemplative. Whatever I willed myself to be would influence my destiny, as well as affecting that of others around me.

Endocrinologist and holistic healer, Deepak Chopra, argued that our intentions and desires wield tremendous potential for self-fulfillment.[32] In fact, many quantum chaos theorists, philosophers, and spiritual leaders have argued that thoughts in themselves can transform reality. In August of 2004, for example, *The Washington Post* published an article on how a small town in Iowa, where many business owners practice formal meditation, had been thriving financially in contrast to surrounding communities, which were struggling economically.[33] Call it introspection, self-reflection, or meditation, the "being" versus "doing" process has become linked with achieving bottom-line results.

I decided to exude happiness at work and to make optimism part of my character. To my delight, I found within me a new wellspring of inner energy that became quite visible to others. Here's a case in point:

Shortly after the layoffs, I was talking to one of my colleagues—let's call her Jill—who was worried about losing her job. She described all the reasons why she might be fired. She was an Asian minority, low on the "totem pole," a woman, less skilled, unassertive, etc. As I quietly listened, she suddenly asked me, "Arthur, why are you always so happy all the time? You're always smiling no matter what, and nothing seems to get you down!"

Surprised at her comment, I shared my parents' counsel with her. It was a simple thing, but shortly thereafter, I noticed that Jill had adopted a similar attitude. Later, she told me that she had repeated our conversation to other colleagues, who had decided to adopt this philosophy, too.

In discussing our choice to "be," Jill and I grew to better appreciate how our destinies and organizational influence depend largely on how we cultivate our inner character, attitudes, and spiritual well-being. For Jill and me, balancing "doing" with "being" led to concrete opportunities to positively influence others. Each seemed like a minor miracle in itself, and reinforced our commitment to grow in practicing spirit-centered leadership.

2. Faith versus Fear

The "being" orientation also helped Jill and me to replace fear with a forward-looking faith, one that created an infectious collaborative climate in our organization. Not long after the layoffs, concerned local managers began searching for ways to restore morale. They announced a brainstorming session, but only three people attended: two managers and one new guy—me.

We kicked around ideas and finally decided to sponsor a group picnic centered on a "county fair carnival" theme. Had I not been consciously trying to function in the "being mode," I might have easily become cynical about our prospects for success due to our timing and limited budget.

By this time, however, I was feeling a spirit of volunteerism along with my positive, optimistic outlook (the "being" mode). As I opened myself to possibilities, I ended up diving head first into actually organizing the picnic. In addition, a little creativity surfaced as I volunteered to create props for our county fair carnival, complete with life-sized cardboard cutouts of various farm animals.

I commandeered an empty conference room for work space, discreetly stuffed my desk drawers with dry-erase markers, and scrounged dumpsters at local retail stores for discarded cardboard boxes. I also brought in felt-tipped pens and a roll of butcher paper from home. Finally, I was ready to begin.

Initially, I worked after hours, but Jill soon noticed my strange activities and confronted me, as she did previously, whereupon I explained my task. Catching the spirit, she offered her assistance, although hesitant about her artistic abilities.

We made overhead transparencies of animal images using one of her daughter's coloring books, and I projected the images onto the butcher paper taped to the conference room wall. With dry-erase markers Jill traced the images from the projection, producing perfectly enlarged drawings of cows, horses, pigs, chickens, rabbits and sheep. We then cut the images out and attached them to cardboard backing.

As Jill and I continued our semi-clandestine effort, one-by-one we were "caught" by other curious employees, and before we knew it, our conference room was bustling with co-conspirators.

One skeptical colleague asked how we planned to ensure that our cardboard animals stood upright in the ground against the wind during the picnic. We had no idea. To my surprise, the next day, our colleague showed up with wooden stakes and a power stapler. With all of the banging noise coming from our conference room "assembly line," it's a wonder anyone in the surrounding offices accomplished any real work.

It soon became necessary to shield management from the mess in our little construction zone. Incidentally, I had hoped that the butcher paper taped to the walls would be thick enough to prevent the dry-erase markers from leaking through it, but I discovered that this was not the case. I spent more than one evening (and into early morning) scrubbing animal images off of conference room walls with soapy water so that nobody would notice!

To this day, if one carefully scans a certain conference room in a particular IBM facility, the faint silhouette of a life-sized giraffe can still be discerned etched indelibly into the wall. I'm not sure why we thought it was an appropriate farm animal, but I think my giraffe won a blue ribbon at the fair anyway. . . .

From this simple idea came even more creative sparks. For example, we produced a life-sized image of a clown, using one of our larger cardboards as backing. Then we cut a hole in the board where the clown's face would have been. During the picnic, we invited our managers to stick their faces through the hole and threw water balloons at them. It was a highly popular feature of the fair!

As we labored together on our animal farm, the sense of connected energy among employees visibly increased. Channeling our efforts also seemed to help us constructively release negative stress, frustration, and anxiety.

Although perhaps childish and trite, that project accomplished a great deal. It helped us to find renewal as a self-organized team. Rather than moping around like down-trodden victims, we became galvanized around mutually shared tasks. Through creative expression and enterprise, we risked bringing our whole, authentic, and spiritual selves to work so that we no longer reflected helpless automatons waiting for the next round of layoffs. Rather, we became inventors and "intrapreneurs," collectively shaping our destinies and having fun in the process.

We forgot about our fears and began anticipating the future with a fresh sense of faith in each other and the brighter possibilities ahead.

Productivity in our jobs began to improve as well. When our new CEO, Lou Gerstner, came on board, he pleaded for an ad hoc group of change agents to spontaneously arise and revitalize the company. This symbolic virtual team became jokingly called "Gerstner's guerrillas."[34] Although our tiny band of animal farm enthusiasts didn't quite see ourselves in this light at that time, I think our efforts symbolized Gerstner's plea for creative transformation.

In fact, although numerous employees at the grassroots level responded to Lou's request, I like to imagine that our team's cardboard cutout cows were actually prophetic—soon our fledgling division rapidly grew into a cash "cow" for the entire company.

3.   *People versus Programs*

As I continued working at IBM, I received increasing responsibilities. I was eventually slated for the company's "fast-track" program to be groomed as a high-potential emerging leader. Along with this designation came rapid promotions, and I was given challenging tasks such as re-engineering a $300-million information technology budget for a 12,000-person worldwide division. Still, through all of this corporate climbing, one of the most valuable lessons I learned in spirit-centered leadership was from those early layoffs—that programs are for people, not the reverse.

As I continued to cultivate the "being" mode and replaced fear with faith, I became increasingly involved in volunteering for extracurricular projects, including planning farewell celebrations for follow-on waves of locally terminated employees and others who voluntarily retired. Often, the honorees expressed gratitude for my efforts during these events, and I realized just how vital it is to acknowledge the dignity of the human spirit, notwithstanding the harshness of many corporate programs that can appear to be economically expedient.

When systems get big, considerations such as these tend to diminish. Nevertheless, I learned that spirit-centered leaders recognize the worth of individuals and honor their enduring interconnectedness in the grand scheme of things.

One of my greatest lessons was to realize *that leadership is not so much about accomplishing tasks through people but about building people through tasks.* Beyond focusing on materialistic objectives, spirit-centered leaders foster a sense of meaning, purpose, and passion in others.

One of our company vice presidents once told me that the key to success in any business is focusing on process. I beg to differ. Through my experiences, I have learned that the power and vitality of any organization rests not just in its programs or processes, but in its people, whose fire in the heart and spirit are reflected in every team member.

As IBM struggled for survival in the late 1980's, the firm opted to focus on programs versus people, emphasizing economic utilitarianism rather than an adherence to its espoused values. Yet, some firms have followed different paths in a similar situation with positive outcomes for both people *and* programs.

After the September 11, 2001 tragedy, for example, while seven of the largest airlines laid off over 15% of their combined employee base, totaling more than 125,000 terminated employees, Southwest Airlines chose to adopt another strategy. The regional carrier actually expanded its operations.[35] The possibility of layoffs never occurred to top company executives. With an in-flight magazine called *Spirit* and a stock symbol of *LUV,* Southwest remained true to its core value of altruism and caring concern for employees.[36]

Similarly, as economies floundered in the southern hemisphere during the 1980's, Brazilian manufacturing firm, Semco, innovated yet another alternative to layoffs. Hailed as one of the world's most unusual workplaces, Semco created cartoon policy manuals and implemented self-selected salaries.

As the country's economic crisis worsened, instead of eliminating employees, the manufacturer assisted workers to launch their own businesses. Employees who tried Semco's "satellite spin-off" program not only became highly successful entrepreneurs but also invaluable resources to Semco as preferred partners and suppliers.[37]

At Silicon Valley semiconductor firm, Xilinx, a longstanding mantra of "layoffs as a last resort" became legendary during the dot-com bust and recession of 2001. While the rest of the industry downsized, Xilinx avoided layoffs by partnering with employees to expand market share and boost productivity, saving over $10 million per quarter in payroll costs and achieving enviably high employee retention rates. [38]

Even when steep pay cuts became temporarily necessary, Xilinx's holistic management philosophy fueled an innovative spirit among employees that continued to strengthen the company's overall efficiency and competitiveness.

David Levine of the Brookings Institution has observed that at least one million employee terminations happen every year in the United States under circumstances in which the company cannot demonstrate a legitimate cause.[39] Conversely, concern for employees found at Xilinx, Semco, and Southwest reflected a spirit-centered leadership that truly valued individuals even under challenging economic pressures.

Spirit-centered leadership can apply even when layoffs become the only viable recourse. For example, when Cisco eliminated 8000 employees in 2001, roughly 16% of its workforce, one organizational psychologist noted that the firm "did it in the most spiritual, humane way . . . I have ever seen, very spiritual."[40]

Corporations don't have to take the organizationally domineering road. Semco and Southwest didn't. Neither did Xilinx or Cisco. Someone once said, "If ever you make a mistake of judgment, let it be on the side of mercy." My experiences helped me to see that we need more mercy in American business.

We frown on monopolies and oligopolies that exist in many other cultures, i.e. oil cartels in the Middle East and Kiretsu in Japan (the tight collusion of government and industry). We tend to tacitly believe in competing based on an ability to provide individual value rather than collective synergy. Yet, such attitudes often become translated into "dog-eat-dog" workplace behaviors that diminish spirit.

Although I am a firm believer in capitalism and the principles of a market economy, there is truth in the call by some leaders to develop a "kinder capitalism" centered in altruistic virtue ethics and a sense of transcendent connections. As companies gradually learn to balance their emphasis on people versus programs, I am convinced that greater community, shared responsibility, and collaboration can ensue, thereby infusing more kindness into our capitalistic market-places and organizational life.

The Call to Serve

Through these early work experiences, I learned that you do not have to be a yogi or a saint to adopt spirit-centered leadership, but you *do* have to recognize that something more significant or transcendent than material, temporal pursuits rests at the root of life's purpose. As we at IBM worked to revitalize our spirits, I observed some co-workers talking about their sense of reliance on something greater than themselves. Often they commented that somebody was watching over them.

By cultivating the "being" mode, building a sense of faith, and recognizing the worth of souls, they acknowledged that a connection exists to something more transcendent in their lives. They felt a closeness to an omniscient provider or power.

Of course, it's well known that trials and tribulations tend to help us see reality through this lens. Conversely, I noticed that some employees who had tied their self-esteem to the company's perceptions of their worth experienced a harder time coping with the layoffs.

Eminent psychologist Victor Frankl approached this idea when he opined that, for many Jews laboring in Nazi concentration camps during World War II, survival required an intense understanding that the human essence is more than just a physical body or cognitive brain. An animating life force invigorates every individual and becomes manifested in our being, conscience, emotions, and purpose.[41]

When we are aware of this, we can learn to tap into it and express it in our daily lives, transcending our challenges and trials whether at work, home, or school. In today's world of tension and conflict, organizational domination may be increasingly prevalent, but leaders can continue helping followers surmount difficulties by centering their leadership on a respect for the spiritual nature within all of us.

As for myself, I was stirred by an appreciation for the "bigger picture" and transcendent connectedness. I vowed to serve and to help others in the difficult days following the layoffs. Robert Greenleaf called this attitude "servant leadership," a vital dimension of spirit-centeredness.[42]

The humility that comes with this attitude can positively influence business results. For instance, service-oriented volunteerism helped me focus on providing quality service to customers. Our division eventually became a top revenue producer for IBM due in part to an adaptation of this principle.

The Hay Group determined that as much as 30% of a company's performance is influenced by its climate, which subsequently affects revenue, efficiency, and profitability.[43] I believe that positive climates can be better fostered and enhanced when altruism or "virtue ethics" coalesce with an attitude of servant leadership.

When Enron and WorldCom collapsed, displacing thousands of workers, some courageous ex-employees refused to become victims and created relief funds to aid colleagues struggling with financial difficulties.[44] This altruistic concern fostered a spirit of service, community, and stewardship characteristic of a higher transcendent awareness and effective spirit-centered leadership.

Revitalizing Spirit-centered Leadership

As I felt my way through IBM's corporate superstructure during those early years with the company, I constantly sought advice on how to proceed. Perhaps the best counsel I ever received was from one of my early mentors, a company vice-president, who told me to simply trust my instincts or intuition.

That intuition pointed toward following a path of spirit-centered leadership. Through my experiences, I have learned that spirit-centeredness is not an ethereal concept. It is *very* real, potent, and transformative in commercial contexts, and it can influence productivity, performance, and marketplace success.

Tom Watson, Jr., who succeeded his father as IBM CEO, had an inkling of this strength as well. In a lecture at Columbia University in 1962, he said that a firm's spirit is more powerful in defining its success than "technological or economic resources, organizational structure, innovation and timing."[45]

Over the ensuing thirty years, the purity of that philosophy became lost on the company. *Doing* replaced *being*, fear overcame faith, and programs dominated people. Still, the imperative persists, and our era has become ripe for a re-emergence of spirit-centered leadership in effective corporate governance across the globe.

I personally found that while formal direction may come from the top, faith, spirit, and altruism can come from anywhere in the organization. Spirit-centered leaders do not have to wield formal positional authority to build courage, community, and collaboration. I didn't have to be an executive to make a difference; I needed the right attitude. I would have many management assignments and responsibilities throughout my career at IBM, but I never had any greater influence than I did as a new hire while rallying the troops to revitalize our traumatized spirits.

Management author Peter Vaill has observed, "All true leadership is indeed spiritual."[46] Consequently, our most urgent challenge is to advance "being" versus "doing," faith versus fear, and people versus programs with altruistic service borne of transcendent awareness. In proceeding thus, a kinder capitalism can ensue where flow replaces force as a dominant organizational ethos.

The imperative for spirit-centered leadership is more urgent than ever. In fact, our collective future depends on it. When leaders reach inward and upward, nurturing their spiritual natures and those of their stakeholders, transcendent forces can be unleashed. These forces can change outcomes, transform companies, and create brighter opportunities—all vital for our survival in an increasingly uncertain world.

7

Courage Under Fire: Standing Firm Despite Fear

Jon M. Corey

The scene: An isolated hilltop in a remote valley in the Republic of Vietnam. The situation: Three young American soldiers preparing to hold off an onslaught of 300 Viet Cong troops headed directly at them. The date: August 17, 1969.

Was this a script for yet another war hero flick? Or, for those standing on that hilltop, would it be a mini-version of the "Dien Bien Phu" massacre that happened to the French years earlier?

My mind was filled with thoughts of doom and valor as I stood with my *ad hoc* two-man command and debated whether or not to give up our tenuous hilltop position. As the commanding officer of these two soldiers, I had been ordered to have them picked up by helicopter and ferried off the mountain top. They had been isolated on duty for six long months in an area no larger than an average kitchen, and it was high time to leave their position for the safety of a rear area.

But I was torn. As an experienced combat arms officer, I now faced a life-and-death decision. Over the years, I've reflected on my actions during this "moment of truth" when confronting battlefields in corporate boardrooms, academic institutions, and government inner sanctums.

However, back on that cut-off hilltop my "two-man command" was resisting orders to evacuate to our main base in the face of the potential attack by a large enemy force. All of us had a tremendous desire to remain and defend this strategic bastion, despite the probability that it would become our "last stand" in every sense of the word.

My dilemma had unfolded during the helicopter mission to pick them up. Gazing out the window, I saw enemy activity below, and I knew that our military personnel stationed in the valley below would soon be in real danger if our strategic outpost—and potential heavy gun position for the advancing enemy—were to be abandoned by us. Innocent villagers would also be killed. Even as our helicopter approached the hilltop, we began taking heavy fire.

Once I arrived at the hilltop to retrieve the two soldiers, the anxious pilot implored my men to board quickly. Yet somehow, I couldn't carry out my orders. The helicopter hovered for what seemed like an eternity as I jumped out and explained the situation to my soldiers. I felt compelled to look each of them squarely in the eyes and ask, "Can you stay on and hold the position?"

Unhesitatingly, they replied, "Sir, we'll stay if you will!" And thus ended the briefest decision-making focus group I had ever chaired!

Our pilot listened, unbelieving. Then, clearly the only sane person on the mountain top, he promptly "pulled power" and left the hill, and us, as quickly as possible.

Once he had gone, all hell broke loose. The three of us were forced to defend our pinnacle against a myriad of assaults for three horrific days and two harrowing nights. We inflicted heavy casualties on a large number of combat-seasoned enemy troops in the process.

Surreal as it was, retreat for our tiny band was impossible. Our intense fighting had become a stubborn, almost suicidal attempt to "save the outpost." We had taken a stand and there was no way out. Later, the Army issued the following Order summarizing the results of my decision that day to stay and fight.

Department of the Army
Headquarters, Americal Division
APO San Francisco 96374
10 February 1970

GENERAL ORDERS
NUMBER 1344
AWARD OF THE BRONZE STAR MEDAL

1. TC 439. The following AWARD is announced.
COREY, JON M, 183-36-0072, FIRST LIEUTENANT, AIR DEFENSE ARTILLERY
Battery G, 55th Artillery, Americal Division Artillery APO 96374
Awarded: Bronze Star Medal with "V" Device
Date of service: 17 August 1969
Theater: Republic of Vietnam
Authority: By direction of the President under the provisions of Executive Order 11046, 24
August 1962

Reason:
For heroism while participating in ground operations against a hostile force in the Republic
of Vietnam. First Lieutenant Corey distinguished himself by exceptionally valorous actions on
17 August 1969 while serving with Battery G, 55th Artillery. On that date, in anticipation of an
attack on Landing Zone Tra Bong, Lieutenant Corey had himself flown to an outlying forward
position to coordinate the activities of an observation team and a searchlight and quad 50
team. Although he had been given the option of abandoning the post prior to the attack,
Lieutenant Corey and his comrades volunteered to remain in the vulnerable position. When
the outpost came under attack from a reinforced North Vietnamese Army company, Lieutenant
Corey directed effective artillery and air strikes against the insurgents, and personally directed a
devastating hail of machinegun and M16 rifle fire against the advancing enemy. His courageous
actions repulsed the enemy's attempt to overrun his position and thwarted their planned attack
on the Tra Bong Base. First Lieutenant Corey's personal heroism, professional competence,
and devotion to duty are in keeping with the highest traditions of the military service and reflect
great credit upon himself, the American Division, and the United States Army.

FOR THE COMMANDER:
OFFICIAL:
T. H. TACKABERRY
Colonel, GS
Chief of Staff
LARRY D. FLOWERS
CPT, AGC
Asst AG

Unwilling and unable to withdraw, and facing a foe with overwhelming force bent on killing us and taking the hill, I learned a lesson that has shaped my military, business, organizational, and academic leadership ever since. As John Wayne simply stated, "Courage is being scared to death, but saddling up anyway." I also recall that someone once said, "Heroes are no braver than normal men, only brave five minutes longer." In our case, five minutes turned out to be three grueling days!

Decisive Factors and Actions

Though strong emotions fueled my decision to stay on the hill, my moment of decision was guided by a quick review of the risks and outcomes. I knew that my emotions had to be set aside in favor of logic, tactics, cunning, and "guts." Therefore, I assessed all our available resources, including water, ammunition, and communications gear, as well as the positioning of our small cache of weapons and mines.

I quickly reviewed the efficacy and viability of our deteriorating tactical situation and a myriad of other vulnerabilities. Foremost in my mind was the specter of us becoming an attractive target for hundreds of highly motivated, combat experienced, and aggressive enemy gunners, sappers, and infantry.

In addition, I had to let our *own* combat forces know that we were still on the hilltop in order to avoid friendly fire. There is a saying that "if the enemy is in range, so are you!" I fully appreciated that wisdom. . . . "Friendly fire ain't!"

Perhaps most important, I had to lift the morale of my two companions as high as possible. I found that maintaining humor while on that hilltop was not only vital to diffusing our tension and anxiety, but also to lifting our spirits. *In humor there is truth* for leaders and teams who dare to embrace it.

Incidentally, media reports of the London train bombings in 2005 also spoke of how numerous British victims exhibited a stoic sense of humor in the aftermath of the terrorist attack as a survival mechanism for coping with the trauma and devastation around them.

Using a similar strategy, we three soldiers moved with precision and unity to overcome almost insurmountable odds. We learned that ability, luck, mettle, and camaraderie were far more important than rank, position, or title.

In the ensuing decades, I found my personal, organizational, emotional, and professional perspectives had been grounded in this particular moment. I had read earlier on a Vietnamese cemetery gate, "Life has a flavor the protected will never know." I now deeply appreciated the wisdom behind these words.

In subsequent business, military, and academic environments, my actions on that isolated Vietnam hilltop would form the basis of numerous leadership and organizational lessons, not the least of which have been the following:

1.   When you have to make difficult, yet effective, decisions under less than optimal circumstances, make sure that your allies know your "position" and expectations.

2.   Know that, in general, emotion tends to win over logic. Therefore, dispassionately evaluate your risks and alternatives—and don't expect any leeway or concessions from the opposition.

3.   Focus on what you can do without dwelling on what you cannot.

4.   "Go for it"—despite the chaos.

First, with respect to "positioning," in the organizational world, a leader must sometimes have to decide if significant problems exist without allowing fear, emotion, or uncertainty to cloud his or her judgment. Leaders must determine:

- If there are any distinctly different options or reasonable courses of conduct available;

- What personal or organizational interests would be affected, one way or the other;

- Whether some measure of relative control currently exists;

- Whether the goal could be achieved with minimal—or reasonable—risk;

- What personal experience or information can assist decision-making;

- Who are the audiences, and what are their positions;

- What it would take to become convincing, effective, and successful.

Second, emotion overrides logic in virtually all organizations. In fact, logic tends to support our emotions and justify decisions *after* we have made them. Without a doubt, logic is manifestly important, but it is emotion that is the nucleus of what we ultimately do or choose not to do.

Whereas logic might tell us not to act against our self-interest, it is our emotions that create the conditions for selfless heroism. As leaders, we must choose wisely to balance these two opposing dichotomies.

Years after my experience on that hilltop in Vietnam, I encountered a similar challenge. Back in the mid-1980s, I was a partner in Seattle with two other management and organizational psychologists. We had been conducting psychological testing for the National Football League (NFL) in support of rookie draft selection processes.

I approached the Seattle Seahawks Players' Association, coaches, and management with a novel idea. I proposed creating a unique "psychological blueprint" of Steve Largent, the premier pass receiver, not only for the Seahawks, but for the entire NFL.

As a future Hall of Fame player, Steve's profile could be the basis for selecting the best future receivers for the team, especially as Steve was planning to retire. While not particularly swift, big, or agile on the field, he possessed something intangible that made him a great receiver. The Seahawks' coaches and management stood to gain an invaluable, precise edge with these elusive mental abilities, skills, personality traits and gems of knowledge, thus helping them to make better draft selections.

By using our blueprint, the Seahawks would no longer have to rely on rookies to simply have "good *shoulders* under their *heads*." Rather, they could ensure that all rookies had "good *heads* on their *shoulders*." Success with this project would lead to tremendous opportunities for the three of us, as the NFL would adopt our services for other teams as well.

After conducting a series of highly satisfactory trials for the Seahawks coaches, management, and Players' Association, my partners and I met with all the stakeholders to decide the details of what promised to be a very lucrative contract.

However, it became apparent during our discussions that the Seahawk staff wanted us to focus on testing and identifying which players would "play when hurt." Their coaching philosophy was to seek aggressive, determined, tenacious, calculating, mean players, regardless of the potential for personal injury. Essentially, we were asked to help with this effort, rather than conduct the originally proposed profiling of Steve Largent as a receiver.

My partners immediately and enthusiastically responded that, yes, we could do this! We'd be happy to help the Seahawks find players who were a cross between Godzilla and The Alien. Everyone in the conference room was elated, riding on an emotional high, and completely enthusiastic about the prospects—everyone except me.

Although I had always been a conscientious risk-taker with a bit more experience in the field than my two associates, I quickly saw the downside to this new testing approach. I asked my jubilant partners if I could have a word with them outside the Seahawks' conference room. To the chagrin of the NFL officials, we excused ourselves and sought some privacy.

Immediately, my partners challenged me, whispering, "*What are you doing!? Have you lost your mind!?*" I responded by asking them if they had any idea how much liability we would have in a lawsuit if we helped the Seahawks pick rookies who would play when seriously hurt or sustaining possibly life-crippling injuries.

As reality reared its ugly head, my colleagues began to recognize the truth behind my words. Of course, it would have been easier to just go along with the crowd, "let emotion win over logic," and jump on the bandwagon to fame and riches. But in the long run, we'd be inviting someone to knock on our office door with a $100-million lawsuit!

Once again, I'd made an instantaneous decision based on a strong gut feeling. Call it emotion-based (I didn't like the lack of ethics involved), but it was tempered with a strong dose of logic. Fortunately, my partners rallied to my position, and we rejected the contract offer, packed up our materials, and went home far wiser, if somewhat chastened.

Third, there is a fine line between courage and imprudence. Leadership in any situation or endeavor should be as focused downward (*e.g.*, my decision to stay with my men at Tra Bong) as much as, if not more than, it is centered upward (*e.g.*, my commanding officer's orders to evacuate the site).

Regarding this third dynamic of demonstrating courage regardless of the odds—even if it means challenging your organization in favor of your subordinates—I offer an example from the sacred ivy-covered halls of academe.

During the 2004–2005 school year, I was one of two Doctoral Program Chairs at the largest accredited university in the United States. In this capacity, I noted that management practices, methods of dealing with faculty, organizational behaviors, and relationships with students at the university were woefully mismanaged across the board, both in my judgment and in that of most of my colleagues.

While my contemporaries would grumble and cite daily university management transgressions, revealing that "we are *not* what we teach," it was apparent that no one was about to try to improve the situation. I sensed that it would take "precipitating a crisis" to win any attention or effect any changes or improvements.

Because the university was conducting doctoral degree programs in such topics as organizational management, business administration, and educational leadership, it allowed for a wide spectrum of *mis*management. Challenging the system was not a good career move for anyone. Actually, it was the organizational equivalent of falling on one's sword.

However, at the end of 2004, I chose to support my colleagues by doing just that: challenging the organization. I distilled into writing the most salient flaws that caused my compatriots and me frequent heartburn. I sent my letter up the university chain of command to what I termed "The Administriviata." Then, I promptly resigned.

My actions generated the expected firestorm, and working conditions temporarily improved to a minor degree. My associates lauded me for my tenacity (all stating that they *should* have done the same thing!), and I subsequently found myself a better professional position.

However, I was the only senior faculty member to take the necessary action. To paraphrase Hamlet, "Unemployment doth make cowards of us all." Still, I had done what I could within my sphere of influence, just as I had done years earlier with compatriots in a different yet similar situation on a dangerous hilltop in Vietnam.

Fourth, we must try to *persevere despite the pandemonium.* Strangely, as my hilltop world in Tra Bong became more and more tenuous by the minute, I remembered a cartoon from my college days. Two serious-looking executives were talking amid large volumes of corporate documents. One said to the other, "Say, how is our Plan B, 'Running and Screaming in All Directions,' coming along. . . ?"

The clear decision that lay before me in that leadership crisis on the hilltop was to "go for it" despite the chaos and danger. When situations mandate it, leaders must be mentally prepared, wholly courageous, and psychologically hardy enough to do what needs to be done.

I had significant leadership experience in "going for it, despite the chaos" while working in the health administration field in the mid-1990s. I was asked to assume the position of Interim Executive Director for a major mental health agency in the Pacific Northwest. It seemed as if the previous Executive Director, using false credentials, had "left town" after running amuck with the organization's accounting, staffing, contracting, credentialing, and servicing functions. Criminal charges were pending, and the entire workforce was angry at this malfeasant leadership, as well as at the Board of Directors who allowed it to happen.

I had been apprised of the situation and accepted the role of "Executive-Level Hired Gunslinger" to straighten things out. I decided on my first day to have a meeting with the entire staff. Every board member was afraid to attend the meeting, as each of them knew I would be facing more of an angry mob than a staff. Everything was in disarray: Funding was in peril, investigations were underway, good people were resigning, and morale was nonexistent. In effect, the agency was going "belly-up."

But from my perspective, the situation was perfect. I could only improve things. However, I did not have the time, opportunity, resources, or penchant to create focus groups, conduct more investigations, or "hand-hold" anyone. Some symbol of stability and leadership had to be established immediately, as several competing and highly influential factions within the organization had emerged over the preceding months.

I felt like Marshall Dillon of *Gunsmoke* facing a fuming and desperate lynch mob. So, I did what needed to be done. Based on my "homework" before my first day on the job, I created a rough working plan. Then, facing the anxious group, I introduced myself, requested order, acknowledged everyone's concern, sought support, and provided an overview of my plan, stating that it wasn't perfect, but it would get us through the next thirty days.

When opposition and grousing flared up, I dampened it fast, telling people to focus on the "here and now," and I quickly fired those who would not comply with my directive. I had no other choice under the circumstances, for I had to rapidly and accurately separate the "capable and willing" from the "resistant and inept." I did this by gaining the initial confidence and respect of that nucleus of good people who almost always exist in every organization.

It worked, but only by sheer force of will on my part; otherwise, the organization would have been shut down. While a common strategy in today's organizations is to ensure that everyone is "on board" and "feels good," sometimes this approach does *not* work, particularly when the situation is urgent. In these circumstances, leaders must take decisive action, even if it means alienating others for a time.

Because I embraced some risk-taking instead of risk-avoidance, I was ultimately hailed as the "great savior" of our health organization. Still, it required a great deal of determination to stay the course amid prevailing chaos and impending calamity.

The Fallout and Lessons Learned

Over the years, I've learned that leaders have a genuine responsibility to work to the best of their capacities for the welfare of those over whom they have stewardship. Harnessing subordinates' and peers' ideas and energies is simply not enough, nor is guiding them successfully if the objectives are poorly conceived, ill-mandated, overly optimistic, or self-serving.

True leaders must provide indisputably capable leadership, *not* merely sound management. As leaders, we must demonstrate character and strength of conviction in all that we do, despite what is generally "expected" according to accepted social or organizational norms.

We must also become role models whom subordinates pattern their lives after, whether inside or outside of the organization. Herein rests our opportunity and solemn obligation.

As leaders, we have the responsibility not only to be role models in a situational, personal, professional, and organizational context, but to inspire *esprit de corps*, character, and strength in ourselves and others. Who knows—in the course of doing so, we might even change a bit of history!

That's what happened to my band of faithful soldiers during our defining moment on an obscure hill in the Tra Bong Valley of

Vietnam. We not only influenced other fellow soldiers (like our helicopter pilot) and protected innocent villagers and fellow soldiers in the valley below, but our actions changed the course of our own lives forever.

Perhaps most important, I learned that if we are to lead greatly, we must find and tenaciously cling to the courage within. With such courage, leaders can even take followers on a journey to Hell and back—and have them eagerly look forward to the trip.

8

Creating an A-Team: The Challenge of Raising the Bar

Harold D. Coleman

Being hired to take on a new position with a new company in a new town is challenging enough. Add to the mix a superior who doesn't want to change, no matter what, and you can end up in a place you never expected.

In my case, I "ended up" in Albuquerque, New Mexico, having only heard of it previously in connection with Bugs Bunny's famous line in which he says, "I should have taken a left turn at Albuquerque." My experience as a new Supervisor in the Systems Management Division of the Contracting and Purchasing Directorate actually became my very own "Albuquerque."

Upon my arrival at my new job, I was told to report to the Director of Contracting, whose organization over the past two years had fared poorly. For some reason, the division had failed to provide customer support, and an absence of awards substantiated this lack of positive performance. Because the Systems Management Division had not performed at acceptable levels, its failure affected the entire Directorate.

I, along with all the Division Chiefs, reported to the Director of Contracting. However, the Deputy Director was the man responsible for the day-to-day internal operations. The Deputy held strong "old-school" convictions and hated change, but he had been outvoted by the Director, who felt that changes were needed to improve the organization's performance and re-establish credibility with customers.

That was where I came into the picture—an outsider new to an organization with the mandate to make things better by changing legacy processes and procedures.

The Contracting and Purchasing Directorate was responsible for providing support and business advice to the parent organization and approximately 200 associated organizations. It handled purchase requests covering a diversity of services, supplies, and construction projects, such as janitorial, lawn, food, and refuse collection services as well as appliances, road repairs, and building renovation projects. Over 25,000 employees worked on our property. It was equivalent to running a small town.

During my first month on the job, I discovered that purchase requests were being processed in an untimely, haphazard manner. The problem was two-fold: Requesting divisions failed to submit purchase requests that accurately described their needs, and no one was auditing the accuracy of the requests. As purchase requests were entered into the system, errors occurred that increased acquisition lead times.

When I presented my findings to the Director and Deputy Director, the Deputy Director flat-out disagreed with me, claiming that the Directorate had won many awards for outstanding customer support. I argued that organizations don't survive by resting on their laurels; customers constantly raise the bar, and purchase requests need to be processed with increasing timeliness and accuracy.

I insisted that, to do my job, changes were necessary; otherwise, I would move on, and the organization could find someone else to "mind the store." I was certainly pleased when the Director sided with my comments and endorsed my position (much to the chagrin of the Deputy Director).

The Road to New Mexico

It all began when a senior official at my company headquarters and the Director of Contracting in Albuquerque were discussing the Director's numerous problems. The Director clearly needed someone to fill a key position in running the Division.

I had worked with the senior official at headquarters for two years on joint projects at our Cocoa Beach, Florida office while simultaneously running two branches of the Systems Management Division. He considered me a prime candidate, so he called me, asking if I was interested in moving to Albuquerque to head the Systems Management Division there.

He was surprised when I informed him that my wife and I were planning to leave the organization and move to Las Vegas.

"I hope you'll reconsider," he urged, and then revealed that the Director of Contracting in Albuquerque had decided that I was the right person for the job. Because I had a great deal of respect for my colleague, I asked him to give me a couple of days to think about it.

My wife and I had contemplated the move to Las Vegas for quite some time, and I relished the thought of neon lights, casinos, and the possibility of getting rich quick. Leaving Florida's sandy beaches to explore western mountains and deserts presented an attractive change of pace as well.

However, when my wife and I discussed the position and its possibilities, we decided to relocate to Albuquerque after all. Besides, Albuquerque was close enough to Las Vegas if we wanted to make periodic visits.

The Assignment Begins

The experience I had gained from my management positions in Florida gave me the necessary background and confidence to tackle my new responsibilities. I knew that the Albuquerque purchase control branch was one of two groups critical to the organization's operations, the other being document products management. These two areas ensured that data was input properly and that documents were distributed efficiently.

But on my first day at work, I learned that the previous supervisor had been in a major car accident and was on a leave of absence, maybe even on permanent disability. Some murmurings in the office implied that the accident was due to stress and fatigue from the supervisor's long hours and overtime on weekends. I began to wonder what I had gotten myself into.

Fortunately, I had employees who were eager for change and happy to have a leader with fresh ideas. I immediately attracted loyal supporters who dove in, analyzing data input documents and determining causes of errors on the "errors list." They pored over procurement notices to evaluate inconsistencies in data outputs as well.

With problems identified thus, the next task was to evaluate root causes. My assessment revealed that nobody in the Systems

Management Division had taken time to correct errors that inevitably occurred in the purchase requests.

Processing purchase requests may sound easy, but this all happened before personal computers were on the scene. Organization-wide data inputs handled by this division were labor-intensive and involved transcribers and key punch operators who processed more than 1,600 inputs per day. Each morning, paper copies of all transactions had to be hand-matched with purchase order files, requiring manual audits for accuracy. Still, while these procedures now seem dated, the lessons I learned about managing change have been timeless.

Leading Change

When I presented my analysis to the Director and Deputy Director, the latter predictably disagreed. Flustered by his resistance to change, I decided to "sleep on it" rather than argue further. As I later pondered over our conversation, the Deputy Director's reaction seemed similar to previous bosses who offered an "it's my way or the highway" approach to collaboration. I gradually realized that if the Deputy Director's attitude had been valid, this company would not be in its current mess, and I wouldn't have been hired to clean it up!

Indeed, it was clearly time for fresh ideas and actions. Prior to my arrival, all employees in the division worked long overtime hours to reduce the backlog of incomplete, error-filled purchase requests and bad system data. As a result, employees were burned out from extended hours. Work had become inefficient. Productivity was at an all-time low.

Now was my moment of decision. I knew I'd be getting resistance from the Deputy Director all the way down the line. Should I accept the inevitable and walk away from this disaster, or take the bull by the horns and try to revitalize the division? I decided to see how things went the next day at the first meeting of my new staff.

The room was abuzz with conversation when I entered. I welcomed everyone and then jumped in. I decided to be candid about the challenge we faced. First, I updated the group on my meeting with the Director and Deputy Director. Then, I explained how important accuracy was in processing purchase requests. I asked my staff for their help to develop processes that would eliminate errors and expedite data entry.

To my relief, my frank, heart-to-heart talk with the team created a rush of enthusiasm! The Directorate had previously established well-defined standards for processing purchase requests, clearing error lists, and improving performance. However, we agreed that for our division to regain credibility, we needed to *exceed* the Directorate's guidelines.

If the rules required that purchase requests be processed within five days, we set a new team goal to process the purchase requests within *three* days. If the Directorate required listing and processing errors within one day, we agreed to process the error listings and notices within *four hours.* For all existing standards, we shortened the processing period in order to achieve better results.

I told the team that for us to succeed, we needed everyone's support. Each team member was important. We committed to working smarter by seeking better ways to perform our work.

In the ensuing days, my team conjured up numerous innovative ideas. Not all of them worked, but I supported everyone's efforts. If things didn't pan out as planned, we simply readjusted and pressed forward.

I also proceeded to meet with the leaders of each department we serviced. Upon introducing myself, I asked for their feedback on organizational needs and expectations, fostering mutual understanding.

A key to my success was meeting leaders at their respective locations versus in my office, which helped set them at ease and build trust.

I met with line employees as well, asking for their advice on how to improve tasks and processes. Everyone was eager to share ideas. I found that actual process owners were the most qualified to make improvements. While not all solutions worked, allowing for penalty-free failures became a key to driving cultural change.

With great pride, I watched my team eagerly and aggressively tackle the error listings and procurement notices, meeting the newly established goals and timelines. When someone completed a task, he or she would rush to help others complete theirs. Work became a cooperative effort throughout the division, and over time, we gained respect and admiration from everyone involved as we delivered tangible results.

Overcoming Resistance

Although we had started to achieve measurable success in bringing the division's performance to new levels, I knew that the Deputy Director had disliked me from the beginning and was watching for an opportunity to discredit my efforts. Since I was the "new kid on the block," stakeholder goodwill would be short-lived if our results proved unsustainable, and my job and reputation were still on the line.

During the analysis process, however, employees began to champion my ideas and to solicit support from their friends in other divisions. They shared information and explained how new processes could improve performance. This enabled me to curtail some resistance from the executive level. My team's enthusiasm for change resonated with other employees and created an upsurge of support.

Likewise, meeting with divisional leaders, customers, and employees neutralized resistance as well. Gathering ideas from the stakeholders involved looking both inward and outward in the organization. As I did, people became eager to embrace change because it incorporated many of their suggestions; they began to own the process.

I also met regularly with the Director and Deputy Director to keep them updated. As quality and timeliness began to increase, the results spoke for themselves. Over time, the Deputy Director had no choice but to support our cause, at least outwardly.

Each small win helped me secure greater confidence in my ability as a change agent and a leader. Loyal followers—the champions I mentioned earlier—were key to winning greater confidence, trust, and credibility, particularly in the eyes of the Deputy Division Chief. Without them, I am convinced that my proposal would not have succeeded.

Helping to Make It Happen

After laying the groundwork with customers and management, my turnaround plan became an exercise in empowering the team and supporting them to make it happen. I was more than pleased when innovations started to proliferate.

One of our key innovations to increase productivity included color codes to track critical purchases. This improved management tracking, significantly decreasing administrative lead-time for priority items from an average of 30.5 days to 16.3 days. Using the color codes, we were able to quickly identify purchase requests requiring priority treatment.

I also implemented a monthly reconciliation process, which allowed us to settle the differences between the data in the system and information submitted by customers. Gradually, the data began to match more closely, which enabled the division to work more efficiently and eliminate delays.

We then focused on more training for preparation of purchase requests, clearing error listings and notices, and educating new hires. We used real case studies of effective and ineffective practices and analyzed buyer and administrator input trends to develop a customer guide on creating purchase requisitions.

Using the guide as a training tool was a resounding success. It produced better customer relations and expedited purchases, sharply reducing errors and saving time and money. We continued training new hires and provided periodic refresher courses throughout the division.

Our staff worked hard to raise their performance, and I put significant effort into ensuring that their work was recognized. To enhance their sense of satisfaction, I created an award recognition program that identified employees' outstanding work during the month, quarter, and year. We also sponsored team and group awards such as the *Tiger Award*, where employees could recognize their peers for outstanding accomplishments and support.

The Results of Credible Leadership

As our flurry of activity boosted the division's performance, raising it from marginal to outstanding, my team's confidence in their work soared. Both individuals and teams began to win numerous awards, raising morale to an all-time high.

Thanks to our educational training program, purchase request submissions became more accurate, which resulted in better customer satisfaction as entry errors decreased. Success bred success, and the improvements skyrocketed. We created even more new processes and procedures to eliminate administrative errors, reducing backlog and the extended overtime hours required.

Perhaps we began to exercise what management consultant Peter Block calls "stewardship," accountability to each other and a sense of shared responsibility.[47] Employees took ownership of the processes because, as Gandhi once advocated, they grew to embody the changes that they desired to see around them.

Employees could see how their input benefited the organization. This gave them a sense of renewed meaning in their work and encouraged them to achieve even greater excellence. Thanks to their efforts, the team eventually eliminated any need for overtime at all. Their attitude had turned from desperation to enthusiasm.

All of this had begun with authentic, credible leadership: a listening ear, honest communication, a vision of possibilities, inspired action, innovation, and teaching followers to lead themselves.

Personally meeting with customers face-to-face at their locations instead of writing letters and memos became one of the most rewarding aspects of the assignment. Customers began to talk more openly about issues that affected them and offered possible solutions. Previously, our Division Chief had scheduled customer meetings at his own office. My new approach was perceived as a huge symbolic gesture, signifying to customers that they were important team members.

This shift rapidly produced dividends. Someone once said, "Treat every customer as if they sign your paycheck, because they do!" That was certainly my philosophy. As the division evolved into a highly efficient and effective operation, employees were recognized and rewarded for their work.

I also received awards for my leadership in transforming this marginally performing group into a paragon of quality service.

Lessons Learned

Reflecting on this leadership milestone, I have realized that certain steps were essential to achieving our goals. These steps can translate well to any company's leadership or management situation, especially when implementing significant change. For example, when confronted with a leadership dilemma:

1. *Assess the problem.* Learn quickly. Use all available data and take the time you need to evaluate alternatives methodically. Examine processes and procedures required to accomplish the tasks. It helps to have prior knowledge or experience of how things could/should function, as this can facilitate a vision of the possibilities.

2. *Involve stakeholders.* I can't emphasize this vigorously enough. Leaders need to consider all factors surrounding the problem, especially stakeholders and the human impact of actions and decisions. Stakeholder involvement aids in developing workable solutions. Be sure to obtain employee and customer feedback, input, and suggestions on how to fix any problem. This ensures buy-in and a successful implementation.

3. *Innovate solutions.* Think creatively and without boundaries. Allow for mistakes and encourage experimentation and risk-taking. However, evaluate all solutions, as fixing one problem could create different ones along the way. This step goes hand-in-hand with soliciting input from all stakeholders. Once the input is received, bringing stakeholders together to discuss the problem can spark new ideas or identify possible issues not previously considered. Dialogue can stimulate creativity that leads to even more solutions.

4. *Overcome resistance.* Resistance can occur from anywhere, but

it is deadly if it emanates from senior management. When presenting a solution, be sensitive with your approach. You can have the best solution to resolve a problem, but if you mishandle its communication, all of your hard work can go up in smoke.

5.   *Implement rapid change.* The implementation stage is where new ideas become reality. One of the best ways to ensure success is to have dedicated, committed team members champion the process. Their involvement during implementation can make or break any solution. Get it together quickly, then let it go, and empower followers make it happen. Give management regular status reports, but move quickly and decisively. Monitor progress and stick with the plan.

6.   *Reward excellence.* Recognize and acknowledge employees for their work. As stated earlier, people are a company's most prized asset. A constant question I asked myself throughout my assignment in Albuquerque was, "What am I doing to show gratitude and reward my team for a job well done?" A little recognition can go a long way. When employees feel valued, they not only embrace change readily, but they bring a sense of loyalty and commitment along with them.

7.   *Be tenacious.* An old Japanese proverb says that "money grows on the tree of persistence." Every solution takes sustained effort and willpower. As leaders, we must stick to our vision and convictions with confidence. If necessary, solicit management or other assistance when dealing with outside influences that need to be resolved at higher levels. But be tenacious. In the case of my team, despite the ups-and-downs of daily operations, we would not settle for less than achieving high performance.

Hitting the Jackpot

Through my assignment with the Systems Management Division in the Purchasing and Contracting Directorate, I learned what it takes to manage change and establish credible leadership. I learned that, while it is human nature to resist change, nothing is insurmountable on the road to success. I also discovered how a little vision and sweat could create a lifetime of positive memories and professional collaborations.

As my team labored to achieve excellence in our small but vital corner of the company, I learned how to build *credibility* by having confidence in my leadership *ability*. Leaders must exude conviction that inspires others to rally around them and champion their cause. Without loyal supporters willing to walk the extra mile with me, it would have been difficult to overcome the resistance I encountered.

To garner support, I had to be confident of my ability to transform the division when I presented my assessment to management. I had to believe in myself and my capacity to effect the changes required.

Moreover, I discovered that to establish credibility, I needed to act with integrity. Doing so set an example for my team. I needed to do what I said I would do and keep my word at all costs, even when it became difficult. My actions reflected my work ethic, which had a ripple effect on my team. In other words, they followed my example by setting new goals that would stretch them, demanding their best efforts to achieve these objectives.

I also gained a new appreciation for the meaning of measuring performance improvements. Business leader, Thomas S. Monson, once said that if we deal in generalities, we will rarely succeed, but if we deal in specifics, we will rarely fail. Likewise, if we measure performance, performance tends to improve. If we measure performance and report it back, the rate of performance tends to accelerate.[48]

The road to improvement for our team involved dealing with *specific* processes, tasks, and roles. Measuring and reporting back on this progress spurred substantial change and transformation.

Finally, I had to model the behavior in myself that I wanted to instill in others. It all boiled down to the Golden Rule: treat employees and stakeholders as you want them to treat you. When we conducted personal meetings with stakeholders at their locations, it sent them a message of respect. As I acted on their ideas for enhancing processes, a spirit of collaboration subsequently ensued that ensured the success of our project.

I have wondered sometimes what would have happened had I not accepted this assignment in New Mexico at the Purchasing and Contracts Directorate. Yes, I might have avoided some angst and sleepless nights, but I would have missed opportunities to practice credible leadership and make a difference as a change agent. I would have foregone wonderful associations and new insights about stewardship, teamwork, and innovation.

My wife and I have yet to experience those flashing neon lights and loud bells, striking it rich in Las Vegas. But I actually found a jackpot of infinitely greater worth, a turning point that transformed our company, and my life, for the better. I found a priceless reward in championing change by following some simple, yet sage, advice from Bugs Bunny, "Take a left turn at Albuquerque."

9

Rebuilding After Tragedy: How One Company Survived 9/11

Ronald Lesniak

On Tuesday, September 11, 2001, a terrorist attack on the United States created a national leadership moment that ignited the emotions of every American. Mayor Rudolph Giuliani encountered his own "leadership moment" when he was called upon to lead New York City. As one reporter described it:

> For weeks afterwards, Mr. Giuliani was more than just a mayor. Day after day, his calm explanation of complicated, awful news helped to reassure a traumatized city that it would pull through, and that someone was in charge. He attended funerals, comforted survivors, urged residents to dine out, and tourists to come in, all the while exuding compassion and resolve, even as the new threat of anthrax emerged. The man who had seemed so finished just a few weeks earlier was now being greeted with cheers wherever he went: Rudy! Rudy! Rudy! [49]

Mayor Giuliani succeeded in his awesome task because he was able to create a galvanizing connection with his fellow New Yorkers, which helped to pull the city through its time of crisis. He acted quickly, decisively, innovatively, and yet with compassion. Many leaders strove to emulate his example in dealing with the aftermath of 9/11, including me.

Most of us will remember where we were and what we were doing on that fateful day. I was in a hotel in Hong Kong in the midst of a two-week business trip. As the CEO of my own company, Teledex, I was reviewing relationships with third party manufacturers in several different countries.

Teledex is a premiere supplier of in-room guest telephones. We invented the telephone with the buttons that connect callers to hotel services such as room service, the concierge, and wake up calls. Over 95% of our business comes from sales to hotels.

I remember it was almost midnight in Hong Kong after a long day of serious meetings and negotiations. I turned on CNN before retiring, hoping to catch a glimpse of what was happening back home. On the screen appeared what I initially thought was a promotion for a new movie, a thriller depicting a terrorist attack on the World Trade Center.

As I watched in numb horror, the telephone in my room rang, and one of my employees asked if I was watching the news. Just at that instant, I saw a live picture of a jet aircraft crashing into the second tower. Unable to believe what I was seeing, I hastily threw on some clothes, rushed out of my room, and went up a few floors to my friend's hotel room where he and a second employee watched, transfixed, as the scenes and commentary in New York unfolded.

We were now desperate for information about our families. As newscasters painted a picture of a potential nationwide attack, I felt helpless, my mind reeling with the implications. I finally reached my wife in Santa Cruz, California. After learning that my family was safe, I told her to withdraw $10,000 from our bank in cash, just in case the national data networks became frozen, making access to money difficult.

Once she reassured me that California was not under attack, I hung up and somehow managed to doze-off as dawn broke in Hong Kong. When I awoke, my fears from the attack began to return. I felt uncertain about what to do, far from home, and very much alone.

By morning, I was considering an immediate trip back to San Francisco. But the airports in the United States were already closing, making travel impossible. I had little choice but to complete my scheduled itinerary in the Far East, then head for home the following week.

It was one of the longest weeks of my life. My imagination worked overtime as every stranger I met seemed like a potential terrorist. I wondered what my family and other Americans were thinking and feeling. I also pondered what this attack would mean to Teledex, whose product was tied to both the hospitality and travel industries. A hollow feeling settled in my gut—a foreboding of grim trials ahead.

The Challenge

Six days after the attack, I was back in the office sorting out our options. Our sales force was still virtually grounded, both by the non-functioning airlines and by our customers, who were in turmoil since the attack. Travel in the United States was stalled, and occupancy rates in hotels were seriously affected.

Within the next two weeks, the extent of the pressure on the hotel industry was becoming clear. Shipment of our products to customers had halted. American business travelers—desperately trying to assess the impact of the attack on their interests—appeared to be meeting exclusively by phone and avoiding travel. All this translated into little revenue and a serious financial shortfall in the making.

Needless to say, as our company moved through October 2001, business deteriorated rapidly. The question of whether or not we would survive began to rear its ugly head. We were in deep trouble.

I had to find a solution to turn things around—most likely a radical one. Spending by hotel customers froze, and occupancy rates fell from mid 70% to mid 60%. No one knew when this freefall would stop.

I could see that the reduced cash flow would eventually compromise our payroll situation. Small companies live from month to month, and payroll is a sacred responsibility. After 15 years in the business, one of my cardinal rules was never to miss a payroll, and I didn't intend to start now.

I knew that I could personally afford a couple of payrolls through my home equity line, and I was determined to keep things going. I also wanted to maintain a profitably run operation, even as our creditors and employees demanded continuous payments.

Dealing with the Team

My task was clear: I had to stop our company's short-term bleeding and plan for its long-term survival. In the spirit of Rudy Giuliani's leadership, I needed to galvanize the faith and trust of my entire team as never before. I gathered my senior staff, and after a candid, heartfelt dialog, we agreed that drastic immediate actions were needed. What emerged was a cost-cutting solution that I had been resisting since the terrible events of September 11: downsizing.

Because I valued my employees above all other assets in the company, I told my staff to search for every conceivable way to cut operating costs. Anything not nailed down was put on the chopping block. We also canceled many of our marketing and trade show expenses, and even walked away from several pre-paid deposits. We froze all hiring activities and suspended bonuses and raises. I knew staff would be disappointed, but we had to keep the ship afloat.

We also asked our suppliers in the Far East for extended payment schedules to give us more operating room. As uncomfortable as this might be for all concerned, our suppliers were going to have to wait for their money.

This decision ran counter to one of my strongest business principles: *Pay your bills on time or lose your vendor's trust*. However, given the extraordinary circumstances, I hoped that my manufacturing partners would stick with me.

To my relief, our suppliers were amenable to working with us on the extensions. I discovered that the pressures of 9/11 were being felt in Asia, too. Our manufacturers needed us as much as we needed them. We all knew that we would have to work things out together.

Indeed, leadership is not only about connecting with one's immediate followers, but fostering trust among all stakeholders, both inside and outside of the organization. I've learned that teams can weather fierce challenges when high-trust environments prevail.

At any rate, once we had determined how much money we needed to move forward, it was then time to face the next challenge: headcount reductions.

The Dreaded Layoffs

For many small companies like Teledex, the lion's portion of their financial investment is in personnel. Reluctantly, we reduced employee benefits, stopped company contributions to the 401K program, and raised medical deductibles. Finally, I had little choice but to reduce headcount.

Leadership involves making tough calls in the midst of uncertainty, often between competing values. As CEO, I found the heartache of employee downsizing one of the most traumatic decisions I've ever had to make. But my staff and I finally assembled the cutback list, which reached our dollar objective.

The best severance packages we could provide were offered to our dismissed employees, and by the end of October, within 45 days of the disaster, our layoffs were completed. However, as we soon learned, this was just the beginning of our battle to survive.

New Directions and New Markets

There are two ways to keep a company financially profitable: by lowering spending and increasing revenues. We had cut spending as deeply as we could. Now, we had to bolster our shortfall in sales.

I decided to focus on new products and markets on a short-term basis. I knew we had to stay within the hotel industry where our 18 years of experience was centered. So, I brought my engineers to the drawing board, and we created ideas for new products.

I shortened the list to two areas that offered the best and fastest approach to enhancing our revenue stream. The top item on our list was to take advantage of a recent experiment with high-speed Internet data that had shown promise. Teledex had developed this product while working with a Taiwanese manufacturer. Since initial testing had proven successful, we decided to move forward.

The product was connected as an add-on underneath our existing telephone. The snap-on piece was simple to install, eliminated unnecessary wires, and kept our telephone's size about the same. To my relief, hotel customers found the product to be valuable, and the industry seemed enthusiastic.

With these positive signs, I decided to take an even bigger gamble. I announced to my sales people that we were going to expand our role into the high-speed service arena, moving from sales of just in-room adapters to selling the entire data system.

This would mean adding special computer hardware and learning a whole new technology, not to mention additional services and support that we had yet to develop. Despite these challenges, I felt good about this market and our expansion.

Of course, while we already enjoyed solid relationships with major hotel decision-makers, we still had to convince them that we could deliver a system backed with effective support services. I decided that we'd do so by engaging third-party vendors in the initial stages for any support requirements.

I told my staff that we had a great little company with great people, and that we understood the definition of the word "hustle": it was a call to action. Everyone jumped aboard and we were soon ready to set sail.

The second potential area of expansion involved developing a new low-end telephone for the economy sector. Teledex had already secured a significant share of the luxury hotel market, but had little presence in the economy sector. If we could capture business in this new market, we'd increase revenues significantly.

There were challenges, to be sure. We faced different competitors and had no existing distribution partners. A successful low-priced product might also negatively impact our luxury business.

Still, I saw genuine opportunity. I was confident that we could develop a low-cost telephone quickly. So I challenged the team to innovate yet again.

As much as I'd like to claim that my leadership inspired my team's creativity, due to the dire circumstances at hand, we innovated as much from *desperation* as we did from *inspiration*. Nevertheless, there is no limit to what can be achieved when leaders leverage human capital to its fullest potential.

With our new products and services, we now had the components necessary to win in the marketplace, or so we thought. Taking risks and innovating strategically eventually paid-off, but only after we added even greater flexibility and tenacity, along with a little luck.

Launching New Products

After our cutbacks and innovations, we watched as the levels of our November and December business continued to fall from a normal $3.5 million per month to below $2 million. But as 2002 progressed, the drop appeared to level off.

We launched "ExpressNet," our new high speed Internet system, and soon realized that, with its service requirements, the offering presented quite an extended learning curve. It also took most of 2002 to find Asian manufacturers willing to partner with us in building it.

When we finally found one, we got lucky and reconnected with an old hotel customer who needed high-speed access. Thanks to our past credibility, we easily won the contract. Not only did this particular customer generate sorely needed revenue, but the deal also attracted a significant amount of positive press, which quickly led to additional customer contracts and rapid international expansion.

My team and I felt as if Lady Luck had smiled on us at last. It was a turning point for Teledex. To me, this scenario also represented a testament to what can happen when a company responds to external challenges by working collaboratively as an integrated and adaptive system—as a "learning organization."[50]

Of course, for Teledex, the learning had just begun. While ExpressNet took off, our new economy sector product, the "Basic Plus," was another story. In my haste to get Basic Plus launched, I underestimated the sophistication of the buyers in this market. I thought that smaller hotels would take less time to purchase technology, but they actually took *longer*, analyzing and comparing alternatives. As our projected sales failed to materialize, I suddenly realized that I had to find a way to sell a potentially un-sellable product!

Repercussions

Tom Peters said, "Test fast, fail fast, adjust fast!" While the launch of the low-end Basic Plus product had initially appeared less risky for the company, it floundered in the marketplace. Yes, we had engineered a slick new telephone, as we had done many times before. However, my gut-level gamble didn't pan out as I had expected.

Now, I had a great product looking for a possibly nonexistent market. In the back of my mind rang the words of a wise business mentor, "The world is littered with great looking products that never sold."

Undaunted, I refocused on finding a new niche for Basic Plus. That's when we uncovered a unique aspect of the European market. Hotels in this region are stratified differently, with smaller properties embracing a boutique approach.

The European market became more accepting of a lower-end model, and we began to see a surge of new business. To keep expenses down, I launched a low-cost delivery approach with our Asian manufacturers. Adjusting fast and acting nimbly did the trick, and we finally found the perfect market for Basic Plus.

As our gradual success rippled through to our manufacturing partners, they became more flexible as well. In the end, teaming with these vendors had been a worthwhile exercise in creating synergy through a symbiotic sharing of ideas, risks, and dedication to long-term success.

Basic Plus and ExpressNet were both huge gambles for Teledex. We had to quickly assess entirely new markets, which demanded agile leadership. We also had to reinvent ourselves into a services business, not just a manufacturer.

Fortunately, we managed to navigate through the learning curve, and today we are building new revenue in this field. Our service organization also holds great promise for the future. In the process, I've learned that effective organizational leadership demands the building of an organic *ecosystem* capable of responding quickly to changing environmental dynamics.

Lessons Learned

The decisions, energy, perseverance, and risk-taking that took place at Teledex after 9/11 clearly demonstrated the need for leadership to create a "breakthrough strategy," a turning point that would lead to successful innovation.[51] The mandate to create new products such as ExpressNet led our engineering team to explore several unique features for our high-speed offering, which gave us a market edge.

This strategy spawned the development of a new combined wired and wireless product that we introduced in 2004. Incidentally, it won "Best Technology Product" at the International Hotel and Motel Trade Show in New York later that year.

As my staff rallied around the need for teamwork, the culture of the organization became electrified, and a noticeable closeness arose among employees. A renewed commitment emerged to achieve our mission of providing high quality products and support.

Following Rudy Giuliani's example of fostering personal connections with New Yorkers, I started making daily "cup of coffee walks" around the business and created reasons for company-wide gatherings where I could speak to our challenges and successes. As personal contact increased, so did a renewed sense of trust between my staff and myself. We all felt a sense of healing, which was much needed after the necessary but difficult downsizing.

Survivability is a strong motivator for making quick leadership decisions. The highly charged emotional atmosphere following 9/11 raised our energy, increased our teamwork, and inspired important gut-level decisions in the midst of tremendous uncertainty about the future.

Teledex's culture was revitalized as we struggled to find success amid chaos by learning to function as a unified *system*—individuals working together for the good of the whole. After fifteen years as CEO, I faced the challenge of helping the company survive the deteriorating, post 9/11 marketplace. I was buoyed by the faith of my employees, our customers, my intuition, and in the knowledge that hard work and perseverance could make a difference.

I also realized that inserting myself directly into the wave of change created my best chance of success. Smooth seas never made skilled sailors, or leaders. So the team and I retrenched and forged ahead together.

Leadership, I learned, is all about execution. There is no substitute for action. Sure, I made some mistakes, but those were part of my leadership lessons. As Rosabeth Moss Kanter said, "A basic truth of management—if not life—is that nearly everything looks like a failure in the middle."[52]

The new products and plans I defined at Teledex were neither right nor wrong until we moved into high gear. This motion created excitement, improved the climate of our company, stimulated the team, and ultimately redefined the destiny of our business.

My moment of crisis during September 11 at Teledex became my moment of resolve. Action-oriented judgment was the call of the day. We embraced an organizational learning curve that turned out to have significant benefits. And because we never stopped trying, we found our way through the uncertainty to new success.

Like everyone else, I had never created a contingency strategy for use after a terrorist attack. In fact, I doubt that planning for this level of crisis makes any sense. My team, however, was able to move forward because of who we were. Collectively, we had a built-in reserve of resiliency, strong relationships, and a company that knew its people, markets, capabilities, and potential.

We enjoyed strong business relationships with customers and suppliers who understood and empathized with the level of our resolve. Thanks to our reputation for solid service, high quality products, and a tenacity that allowed us to change and move forward, we created the customer loyalty we needed to launch our products and to stay in the game.

Just as Mayor Giuliani rebuilt the spirit of New York in the shadow of a terrorist attack, this same incident created a chance for my team and me—now leaner but wiser—to rebuild our company and move with increasing confidence into a new era.

10

Risking It All: The Power of Corporate and Community Partnership

Carolyn Salerno

The sun was warm and bright as I walked on the southern California beach that April afternoon in 1997. But despite the beauty of the scenery, I knew I could put it off no longer. I had to make a decision whether or not to accept the compelling challenge that had been presented to me earlier that day.

I knew two things with certainty: If I failed, not only would my current job and professional credibility be shattered, but my employer's reputation could also be deeply tarnished. At the same time, I understood that more than 500 children and their families were depending on me to turn their lives around. Was I up to it?

A Precarious Situation

At that time, I was employed by Science Research Associates

(SRA), a division of McGraw-Hill, the largest pre-K-12 educational publisher in the United States. I was responsible for sales in public, charter, and private schools for five Southern California counties, from Los Angeles to the Mexican border.

My experience made me the right person for the job. I had earned advanced degrees and both elementary and secondary school teaching credentials, specializing in educational administration and reading instruction. I also had a dozen years of public education teaching experience, three years operating a private reading clinic, and seven years of part-time teaching in advanced degree programs in education, leadership, management, and diversity in California universities.

But never before had I been presented with a challenge as demanding as the one that the President and the CEO of the San Diego Urban League, Mr. McWilson and Mr. Johnson, had handed to me a few days earlier. Would I help them turn around the academic performance of 500 students at the Johnson Elementary School and raise the student's dismally low reading scores to a level where they could improve their overall academic performance?

At the time, school improvement plans allowed a school four years to meet the State's goals. But after three consecutive years of seeing most of its students score below the 50th percentile on standardized tests, Johnson Elementary school had only one more year to improve before the State stepped in to "help" with its administration.

Now, the President and the CEO of the Urban League were fighting for the future of the children at this school. These children lived in a low socio-economic community in San Diego and were 98% African-American. Their parents struggled to provide for their families and, despite loving their kids and wanting the best for them, were often not able to provide a home environment where their children could acquire the early reading skills they needed to succeed in school.

The San Diego Urban League, a community-based organization, decided to take on the challenge of linking 500 underprivileged students with the largest educational publisher in the nation as part of its mission to bring this school social and economic equality. I represented the bridge to that link.

Selling the Vision

When that life-changing call came from Mr. McWilson in April, asking me to join with the Urban League to transform the students' reading test scores at the Johnson Elementary School, I was completely taken aback. I told him I would consider his proposal and get back to him in a few days.

I immediately ran Mr. McWilson's plea past my manager at SRA/ McGraw-Hill and was told, "Send me a proposal that shows how much money this sale will generate, minus the costs per student, and the reasons why this socially responsible project will be valuable to the company and community."

I agreed to take on this feasibility analysis and fax it to him within the week. In the meantime, Mr. McWilson also asked for a feasibility report. To both, I presented an argument that publicly traded firms sponsoring socially responsible programs improve their stock prices because the public supports such efforts. This was a strong argument for taking the risk. But my manager and I both knew that if I failed to get the desired results, our company would lose hundreds of thousands, if not millions, of dollars—not to mention priceless credibility.

Although the curriculum I suggested had significant supporting research and was touted as the best on the market for teaching literacy skills, it would now be subjected to a harsh, real-world test. In addition, if the threat of possible failure wasn't enough, I learned that the materials could not be fully funded by the State Board of Education (SBE) because they didn't conform to SBE standards. The Charter School's budget would have to pay for the expensive curriculum.

Accepting the Challenge

I knew in my heart that this curriculum *would* work. Even so, this project was a risk because entrenched bureaucratic attitudes and fear of change make educational reform one of the most difficult arenas for substantial transformation. Numerous elements would have to fall into place:

- The school principal would have to agree with my plan and support my recommended changes,

- The teachers would have to buy-in to the new curricula and be trained in it,

- I would have to hire consultants with program expertise and a teacher's mentor/coach,

- The parents would have to trust my direction of their childrens' education,

- More teachers would have to be hired,

- I would have to find a way to encourage the teachers and administrators to take ownership of the change, and

- The organizational and educational structure of the school would have to change.

Furthermore, the results of this project would be reported by the media, on the Internet, and possibly by educational and business trade journals. I would have no hiding place. While I worked on this project, I would also have to cover my territory and continue to make my annual sales quota for SRA/McGraw-Hill.

That's how I ended up walking along the beach, letting the rhythm of the Pacific waves soothe me while I contemplated the situation and prayed for guidance, as I often do when faced with challenges. Within three days of Mr. McWilson's initial request, the answer became clear: I'd researched, lectured and written about this subject for years. The time had come to prove that I knew what had to be done to improve the literacy levels of children in one year; it was time to "walk the talk." This was my personal leadership moment.

I knew I would also have to extend that leadership to the other people involved, to those who would make my plan for the school a reality. Could I do that? I truly didn't know. But I wanted to try, and so I committed myself to doing whatever it took to turn around Johnson Elementary.

That was in June. With just under three months before school started, I called Mr. McWilson, accepted the task, and plunged in.

The Work Begins: A Labor of Love

In preparing my proposal to make Johnson Elementary a Charter School, I had learned that about 87% of the students had scored below the state's acceptable level for English. I also understood why the Urban League had targeted the school for improvement: it represented truly oppressive social and economic inequality.

There were many conflicting factors at work. For example, Mr. McWilson shared with me his appreciation for the kind-hearted principal who knew the name and family of every child in the school, and the teachers who cared about their students' progress.

But we also talked about why these children had fallen behind in their educational journey—the "blame points"—including parents, curriculum, teachers, training, funding, administrators, school board, instructional strategies, political agendas, limited opportunities, parochial focus on top students, and standardized test biases.

As a result of our talks, I came to realize that McGraw-Hill and I represented hope for a better future to these children. In turn, this rising generation represented our hope for a better world. They were tomorrow's potential leaders, and I had been given the opportunity to make a difference for them at this one critical moment in their life's journey.

An enormous sense of responsibility emerged. I knew that I had to have unshakable faith if I were going to build a bridge across such a wide chasm. These discussions quietly fueled my determination to do the best job I could for these children. I pledged to do everything in my power to see that they succeeded during the coming school year, passed the standardized tests, established a solid foundation for the future, and met expected educational goals.

A great deal of tension already existed around the school's performance and there were concerns that this change would create more. The community was upset that the school had let the situation deteriorate so seriously and for so long. There was also tension because the Urban League Board would now administer the school's funding from federal, state, and local sources. Teachers were afraid that any move from a public school to a charter school might lose them their seniority or benefits. They resented an outside consultant telling them how to teach their students as well.

I knew that if this project were to succeed, these tensions would have to be diffused by creating solid, honest relationships with all parties involved. I began with the parents.

Building Relationships of Trust

The Urban League had called a parents' meeting, and I was to be the guest speaker. I was nervous. The meeting had already begun when I arrived, and I could sense the thick air of skepticism among the parents and community leaders in attendance. Why would these parents trust me with their children's education? Why would they believe that I, an outsider, would do what I said I would, or that my plan could improve their children's performance?

As I offered my plan for change, everyone responded respectfully, but I had the feeling that they had heard many such plans before without results and were doubtful that I could make the desired progress in one year. A few attendees awkwardly asked prepared questions. Then, suddenly, an argument broke out between two attendees, and I was promptly shuffled from the room. So much for relationship-building!

In July, I began working with the teachers. From my first assessment, I knew that the materials the teachers were using didn't work, so everything had to be changed. I changed the bell system, number of students and assistants per classroom, training classes for the teachers, and literature in the school library and classrooms. I also created schedules for ability groupings, recesses, lunches, and staff meetings. The daily instruction I designed was grounded in behavioral, social, personal, and cognitive learning theory and instructional technologies. Adequately describing it all could fill volumes.

Understandably, most of the teachers were less than enthusiastic. I spent a great deal of time networking, educating, presenting, entertaining, showing and explaining how and why the new program could make a difference. I also engaged a new administrator to coach and mentor the teachers.

Ms. Kasendorf, our new coach-administrator, monitored the progress of each class carefully. If progress was slow, she would intervene with training, facilitation, and coaching. Several of the teachers didn't like having the performance of their classes monitored on a regular basis, and they resented having to follow scripted lessons. Although the principal sent a memo reminding the teachers that the instructional program was designed for student improvement and not for their appreciation, teachers lamented the lack of time for more creative and spontaneous instructional opportunities.

With such frustration among the teachers, we called a coaching meeting after school to hear their issues, concerns and challenges. We then offered explanations and presented information about the unique development of the program. Still, despite my expertise, the teachers didn't trust outsiders, especially a consultant chosen by non-educators (and a publisher's sales rep at that!).

Notwithstanding, my task was to provide the best instructional program available based on research and to give the children skills to read and learn in seven short months. I invited expert consultants to provide testimonials and sage advice. Several of these consultants continued to visit the school and offer support throughout the year. I also arranged visits by other principals who had used this curriculum in their schools successfully.

McGraw-Hill approved scholarships to send three teachers to special training. Not only would they learn how to implement the program in their classrooms, but they would pass their knowledge on to the other teachers. I wouldn't be able to be at the school every day, and if the teachers were going to take ownership, I needed to stay away. The teachers had to know how to continue without my participation—which would reveal how effective a leader I had been. During the school year, I called Ms. Kasendorf weekly, and when I necessary, I paid a visit to the school.

Gaining Momentum

In fact, I hadn't anticipated how successful the program would be. My original proposal budgeted $120,000 for workbooks, storybooks, and textbooks for 500-plus children. As it turned out, the students quickly ran out of books to read at the grade level in which they began. Once children began to gain missing reading skills, they improved so quickly that they tried to read everything they had missed.

I remember a story about a young student who had just learned to read. He walked so slowly down the hall after class, stopping to read all of the signs posted in the halls, that a teacher asked him what he was doing. He responded that this was the first time in his life he had ever been able to read the posted information, and now he actually knew what was going on at his school.

When I learned that a few of the students completed a whole year's proposed program in less than two or three months, there was no time to speculate on how many others had simply stopped reading at the starting level because of limited reading materials. In a way, this was a "good problem," since it showed that the program was working, creating strong readers who loved to read.

My company sent over the few books that we thought we needed, but within four months, it became obvious that we would need many, many more. In fact, we needed far too many to accommodate on my limited budget, and teachers were stopping me in the halls and calling me at home to tell me that they needed more books for students.

I contacted my manager and explained the situation. Knowing the importance of the project to the company, McGraw-Hill came through with another $10,000 worth of books. This was above and beyond paying to send the three teachers to training camp, plus the coaches' and consultants' salaries. In the end, their donations probably totaled more than $100,000. The link between the school and my organization was making a real difference in the lives of students.

Mitigating Threats and Dancing *Fast!*

Despite all of my careful planning, the project did not always run smoothly. I remembered that old saying: Anticipate the worst, because what can go wrong *will* go wrong! Glitches threatened the school's progress all along the way. For instance, one teacher who had extensive experience with this program, and whom I had hired personally, walked away from the school one day with no explanation, leaving his class in line outside the classroom door.

Another time, the day before classes started in September, I waited eagerly at the school for the truck to arrive with all the books. It did, and all the book boxes were placed along the wall in the library. When school started the next day, I found that no one had been assigned to open the boxes and move the books into the classrooms.

It had never occurred to me that I had to plan this detail, too! I went to my car, changed into jeans and tennis shoes, and went to the library to unpack the books. I called school custodians and teaching assistants in during breaks to take books into the classrooms.

Perhaps the biggest glitch happened in February. All the teachers in the San Diego school district went on strike, including the teachers at Johnson Elementary. I was horrified. The students had been doing so well, and now this walkout threatened every bit of progress they had made. But we found a solution. Since the curriculum was closely scripted, substitute teachers and parents were asked to come in and lead the classes. Many of them accepted our invitation for the benefit of the children.

While I didn't cross the picket line, since I had to maintain my link with the teachers, Ms. Kasendorf volunteered to do so. And she did, every day for the three weeks of the strike. We did the best we could with a very difficult situation, but I feared that this situation had ruined any chance we had of sufficiently improving test scores.

Even with all these problems, there was one wonderful highlight for me. A kindergarten teacher stopped me in the hall one day to say, "Thank you." She reported that for the first time, her students were reading before the winter holidays, thanks to the new program. It was wonderful to receive her acknowledgment, but while I had provided the information, she was the one who had taught the kindergarteners to read.

The Moment of Truth

Finally, in May, the students took their standardized tests, and I practically held my breath for weeks until the principal called to tell me that she had the final scores. She said that some were good and some were not so good. I rushed to her office where Mr. McWilson and Mr. Johnson were already there. They watched silently as I pored over the scores for the fifth and sixth graders. Tears began welling up in my eyes as I realized they *hadn't* reached the level of improvement I had expected. I had failed. I felt my heart breaking.

But then, someone said, "Look at the other scores." So I read the scores of the younger students, and 96% of them had all reached grade level and exceeded the fiftieth percentile! I let out a sigh of relief. After some excited discussion, we concluded that the older students had missed more years of education than the younger ones, and would thus take longer to improve.

To everyone's delight, it turned out that Johnson Elementary had made the grade! There would be no consideration of government intervention the next year, and the administration now had a program that worked. My plan had succeeded! The team of administrators, teachers, consultants, and specialists had taken ownership of the program and successfully guided students to improve their academic performance.

Leadership Lessons

Although this leadership challenge took place several years ago, schools and communities across the nation experience the same literacy challenges and apply similar strategies today. The success of any program depends on the community, school leadership, and student strengths and needs.

While educational organizations, in many ways, reflect a different business model from commercial businesses, the leadership and management skills required for success are based on the same principles:

- Dedication to a common mission and vision,

- Engaging in collaborative discussions,

- Working together via meaningful and enjoyable experiences as a community,

- Implementing change in a timely manner,

- Effectively managing resources,

- Contingency planning,

- Implementing ongoing assessment, coaching, and process monitoring,

- Supporting an emotionally positive learning environment based on knowledge acquisition, and

- Being willing to move with and beyond politics.

For me, accepting such a challenge to make a difference took great passion, a connection with the moment of opportunity, a belief and confidence that it could be done, a willingness and determination to ignore the fear of failure, an inner spirituality that would drive the mission, and the courage to take the chance. I experienced all of this firsthand in my year at Johnson Elementary, partnering to educate a new generation of leaders.

Biographies

Peter Amato is a pioneer in the field of integrative medicine. He founded both the Inner Harmony Wellness Center and the Center for Integrative Medicine in Pennsylvania, among the first and foremost of their kind in the nation. Peter is a meditation and yoga teacher with certifications from Deepak Chopra, Jon Kabat-Zinn, and Yogi Amrit Desai. He is also a student of Thich Nhat Hanh, world-renowned Buddhist monk and Noble Peace Prize nominee. Peter worked with and received blessings from the Dalai Lama and is a member of the Board of Regents of Bastyr University as well as a board member of the Clearbrook Foundation. In addition, he serves with Andrew Weil on the board of the Foundation for Integrative Medicine at the University of Arizona.

Gary Bodam is Vice President of Human Resources and Organizational Development for Stuart C. Irby Co., a leader in electrical wholesaling. Previously, he was Managing Partner with SkillsNET. Gary has had over 25 years of international experience in executive assignments with companies such as GE, Johnson & Johnson, Polaroid, Thomas & Betts, and Acuity Brands. He has played key roles in almost 30 mergers and acquisitions. Gary lectures internationally on knowledge management and has a Doctorate in Organizational Leadership from the University of Phoenix, as well as a Masters in Management from Webster University. He teaches human resources, human capital development and transformational leadership at the university level.

Martin J. Boyle is CEO of the International Protection and Investigation Agency. His firm provides corporate security services, bodyguard and executive protection, counter terrorism support, computer security systems, and protection against workplace violence and white collar crime. He is a former member of the Jersey City Police Department and has had more than 25 years of experience in corporate security with one of the world's largest package carriers. Marty is a Black Belt in Tae Kwon Do, Certified Bodyguard, Licensed Private Detective, Certified Fraud Examiner, and Level III Certified Homeland Security expert. He has a B.S. from Nyack College, an MBA in Global Management, and a Doctorate in Leadership from the University of Phoenix.

Rick Brydges is an entrepreneur, educator, consultant, author, and publicist. He is the Executive Director for the Institute for the Advancement of Leadership, Academic Chair and Lead Faculty for Graduate Strategic Management at the University of Phoenix, and Chief Strategist for ARC Leadership Group, Inc. His academic background includes a B.S. in Engineering from the US Naval Academy, an M.S. from the Naval Postgraduate School at Monterey, an MBA from the University of West Florida, and an Ed.D. in Leadership Studies from the University of San Diego. He currently serves the Chair of Global Business Leadership for the International Leadership Association, a forum for exchanging ideas and experiences on business leadership.

Harold Coleman serves as a Program Integration Manager in the Launch Services Program at NASA's John F. Kennedy Space Center in Merritt Island, Florida, where he provides technical and business expertise on major space program initiatives. He earned a B.S. in occupational education from Wayland Baptist University, an MBA, and a Doctorate in Organizational Leadership from the University of Phoenix. He began his career at NASA's Goddard Space Flight Center, Greenbelt, Maryland, where he rose to assume leadership responsibility for an organization that managed over $1.5 billion in cooperative agreements for the company. Harold and his wife, Janice, reside in Titusville, Florida. They have one son, four daughters, and seven grandchildren.

Jon Corey is a professor at Grand Canyon University and the University of Phoenix. He has extensive global experience in providing project management, academic, research, and technical leadership for many international corporate, government, and educational organizations. Jon also has extensive military combat and intelligence experience, and he has served as Co-Chair of Doctoral Programs in Organizational Management and Leadership, Health Care Administration, Educational Leadership, and Business Administration for the University of Phoenix's School of Advanced Studies. He is currently developing a doctoral program in "National Homeland Leadership and Security" in partnership with the U.S. government and State of Arizona.

Claire Gerus has been a publishing professional for more than 25 years. She has been an editor-in-chief of two publishing houses and acquired and edited books for eight major publishers, including Rodale, Random House, Doubleday, Wiley, Kensington, and Adams Media. As a journalist in Toronto, she wrote award-winning cover stories for Canada's top news magazines, including Macleans, Toronto Life, and Canadian Business. Her corporate work includes writing and editing annual reports for clients such as Shell Oil, and teaching corporate communications at Fortune 500 clients such as Procter & Gamble, Prudential, Aetna, Kelloggs, and IBM. Claire attended New York University and received a B.A. in English at Southern Connecticut State University.

Arthur Jue is a Director of Human Resources and Leadership Development for Hyperion Solutions, Inc. and has 20+ years of IT technical and managerial experience in Fortune 100 companies. He also serves on the board of directors for educational and financial services organizations. Arthur has a Doctor of Management in Organizational Leadership and an MBA with emphasis in Technology Management. He attended BYU and received a B.S. in Marketing with a Music Minor from San Jose State University. Arthur has participated in leadership programs at the London Business School, Harvard, and Oxford. He serves on the University of Phoenix faculty, has been a missionary in New Zealand, is an Eagle Scout, and enjoys playing the violin.

Ronald Lesniak is Founder and CEO of Teledex Corporation, the largest manufacturer of telephones in the luxury hotel industry with customers in over 125 countries. His firm has been honored twice as one of the 100 fastest growing companies in Silicon Valley, California. Ron has a Doctor of Management in Organizational Leadership from the University of Phoenix, an MBA from Loyola University of Chicago, and a Bachelor's in Electrical Engineering from Marquette University. His professional background includes numerous technical, marketing, and managerial positions at ROLM, GTE, and ITT. In addition, he is the recipient of three US Patents. Ron is an avid musician, collects art, and enjoys riding motorcycles in his spare time.

John Lohre is President of the Wealth Management Division at Mid-Wisconsin Financial Services. He has been a banking executive for over 30 years at institutions such as Bank One, US Bank, Johnson Bank, and Port Washington State Bank. His career spans many disciplines, including commercial real estate finance, in-house corporate legal counsel, acquisitions and mergers, corporate and commercial banking, private and retail banking, wealth management and trust services. He teaches at Marquette University's College of Business, and has a Bachelor's in Civil Engineering, an MBA, and a JD from Marquette University. John is a member of the Wisconsin Bar Association and is a Director of the Milwaukee Estate Planning Council.

Peter Ressler and Monika Mitchell Ressler are partners in a Wall Street search firm specializing in Institutional Debt & Equity, Sales, and Trading. They serve some of the most influential market makers in the financial industry. Peter graduated from Cornell University in Business and is an active member of the World Business Academy. He is also a volunteer firefighter in New Jersey. Monika's background includes serving as a public relations executive and theatrical producer in New York City. She has a degree from the State University of New York, is a member of the National Women Executives Council, and is a volunteer for Hospice Care of Long Island. Peter and Monika travel and lecture widely on business ethics, money, and spirituality.

Carolyn Salerno has 30 years of experience in the field of education, sales, marketing, management, and consulting. She was a sales representative for IBM and McGraw-Hill publishing for 13 years. Carolyn has also been the owner and director of an educational business. She is a director at the Institute for the Advancement of Leadership and serves on the University of Phoenix faculty, where she was instrumental in co-developing an interdisciplinary doctoral program in Organizational Leadership. Carolyn has co-authored a book on cultural democracy and co-facilitated leadership among high school students in a developing country. She earned a doctorate in Educational Leadership from the University of San Diego.

End Notes

1 Cohen, E., & Tichy, N. (1999, September). Operation leadership. *Fast Company, 27,* 280.

2 Tichy, N., & Bennis, W. (2006). *Judgment: The essence of leadership.* New York: HarperCollins.

3 Kennedy, R. F. (1966). *Day of Affirmation Address.* Capetown, South Africa: University of Capetown.

4 Azarian, A., & Skriptchenko-Gregorian, V. (1998). *Children in natural disasters: An experience of the 1998 earthquake in Armenia.* [The American Academy of Experts in Traumatic Stress]. Retrieved May 27, 2006, from http://www.aaets.org/article38.htm

5 Rost, J. C. (1993). *Leadership for the twenty-first century.* New York: Praeger.

6 Roosevelt, T. (1910, April 23). *Citizenship in a republic: The man in the arena.* Sorbonne, Paris: University of Paris.

7 Diggles, M. (2005). *Mout St. Helens – from the 1980 eruption to 2000.* [U.S. Geological Survey Fact Sheet 036-00]. Retrieved May 27, 2006, from http://pubs.usgs.gov/fs/2000/fs036-00/

8 Cooper, R. K., & Sawaf, A. (1998). *Executive EQ: Emotional intelligence in leadership and organizations.* New York: Berkeley Publishing Group.

9 Lombardo, M. M., & Eichinger, R. W. (2006). *The career architect development planner* (4th ed.). Minneapolis, MN: Lominger Limited, Inc.

¹⁰ Cooperider, D. (1996). Resources for getting appreciative inquiry started: An example OD proposal. *Organization Development Practitioner, 28*(1-2), 23-33.

¹¹ Schmid, F. A., & Emmons, W. R. (2000, May). Bank competition and concentration: do credit unions matter? *Review, 82*(3), 29-42. [Federal Reserve Bank of St. Louis].

¹² Vaill, P. B. (1996). *Learning as a way of being: Strategies for survival in a world of permanent whitewater.* San Francisco: Jossey Bass.

¹³ As cited in Roberts, W. (2002). *The best advice ever for leaders.* New York: MJF Books. [p. 15].

¹⁴ Harari, O. (2002). *The leadership secrets of Collin Powell.* New York: McGraw-Hill.

¹⁵ Barker, J. (1992). *Paradigms: The business of discovering the future.* New York: HarperCollins.

¹⁶ Frankl, V. (1984). *Man's search for meaning* (3rd ed.). New York: Washington Square Press. [p. 86].

¹⁷ Krell, D. (Ed.). (1993). *Martin Heidegger: Basic writings from being and time (1927) to the task of thinking (1964)* (Revised and Expanded Edition, 41-87). San Francisco: Harper San Francisco. (Original English translation published 1962).

Donohoe, J. (1998). Genetic phenomenology, intersubjectivity, and the Husserlian account of ethics. (Doctoral Dissertation, Boston College, 1998). *Dissertation Information Service* (UMI No. 9828022).

¹⁸ Yeats, W. B. (1968). The second coming. In S. B. Greenfield & A. K. Weatherhead (Eds.), *The Poem, An Anthology* (pp. 309-310). New York: Appleton-Century-Crofts. (Original work published in 1922).

¹⁹ Loomis, C. J. (1993, May 3). Dinosaurs? *Fortune, 127*(9), 36-42.

²⁰ Maney, K. (2003). *The maverick and his machine: Thomas Watson, Sr. and the making of IBM.* New York: John Wiley & Sons. [p. 55].

²¹ Watson, T. J. (1987, August 31). The greatest capitalist in history. *Fortune, 116*(5), 24-34.

²² Watson, T. J. (1963). *A business and its beliefs: The ideas that helped build*

IBM. New York: McGraw-Hill. [McKinsey Foundation lecture series, Graduate School of Business, Columbia University].

23   Bennis, W., & Nanus, B. (2003). *Leaders: Strategies for taking charge.* New York: HarperCollins. [p. 70].

24   Watson, T. J. (1963). *A business and its beliefs: The ideas that helped build IBM.* New York: McGraw-Hill. [McKinsey Foundation lecture series, Graduate School of Business, Columbia University].

25   *Ibid.*

26   Sherman, S. (1994, October 3). Is he too cautious to save IBM? *Fortune, 130*(7), 78-83.

27   As cited in Jue, A. L. (2004). Towards a taxonomy of spirit-centered leadership as reflected in phenomenological experiences of entrepreneurial leaders. (Doctoral Dissertation, University of Phoenix, 2004). *Dissertation Information Service* (UMI No. 3136139). [p. 446].

28   *Ibid.*

29   Hatch, M. J. (1997). *Organization theory: Modern, symbolic, and postmodern perspectives.* New York: Oxford University Press. Morgan, G. (1998). *Images of organizations (Executive ed.).* San Francisco: Berrett-Koehler.

30   Jue, A. L. (2004). Towards a taxonomy of spirit-centered leadership as reflected in phenomenological experiences of entrepreneurial leaders. (Doctoral Dissertation, University of Phoenix, 2004). *Dissertation Information Service* (UMI No. 3136139).

31   Linsky, M, & Heifetz, R. A. (2002). *Leadership on the line: Staying alive through the dangers of leading.* Boston, MA: Harvard Business School.

32   Chopra, D. (1994). *The seven spiritual laws of success.* San Rafael, CA: Amber-Allen.

33   Lydersen, K. (2004, August 9). Iowa town booms on eastern ways. *The Washington Post,* p. A03.

34   Ransdell, E. (1997, October/November). IBM's grassroots revival. *Fast Company, 11,* 182.

35   Patsuris, P. (2002). Layoff tracker archive. *Forbes.* Retrieved May 28,

2006, from http://www.forbes.com/2001/09/10/bodycount-archive.html

36 Jue, A. L. (2004). Towards a taxonomy of spirit-centered leadership as reflected in phenomenological experiences of entrepreneurial leaders. (Doctoral Dissertation, University of Phoenix, 2004). *Dissertation Information Service* (UMI No. 3136139).

37 Semler, R. (1993). *Maverick*. New York: Warner Books.

38 Xilinx. (2006). *A legacy of leadership*. Retrieved May 28, 2006, from http://www.xilinx.com/company/about/spirit_HR.pdf

Barnes, E. S. (2003, July). No-layoff policy. *Workforce Management*, 96-99. Retrieved May 28, 2006, from http://www.workforce.com/section/09/feature/23/47/45/index.html

39 Levine, D. I. (2000). *Reinventing the workplace: How business and employees can both win*. Washington, DC: Brookings Institution.

40 Wong, W. (2001, March 9). Cisco to cut up to 8,000 workers. *CNet News*. Retrieved May 28, 2006, from http://news.com.com/2100-1033-253852.html

CNNMoney. (2001, April 16). *Cisco warns again*. Retrieved May 28, 2006, from http://money.cnn.com/2001/04/16/technology/cisco/

Jue, A. L. (2004). Towards a taxonomy of spirit-centered leadership as reflected in phenomenological experiences of entrepreneurial leaders. (Doctoral Dissertation, University of Phoenix, 2004). *Dissertation Information Service* (UMI No. 3136139). [p. 507].

41 Frankl, V. (1984). *Man's search for meaning* (3rd ed.). New York: Washington Square Press.

42 Greenleaf, R. (1991). *The servant as leader*. Indianapolis, IN: The Robert K. Greenleaf Center. (Original work published 1970).

43 Watkin, C., & Hubbard, B. (2003, November). Leadership motivation and the drivers of share price: The business case for measuring organizational climate. *Leadership & Organizational Development Journal, 24*(7), 380-386.

44 Bowser, B. A. (2002, January 28). Enron update. *PBS Online NewsHour*. Retrieved May 28, 2006, from http://www.pbs.org/newshour/

bb/business/jan-june02/enron_1-28.html

Silverman, B. (2003, June 13). A little fund makes a big media splash. *Smallbusinessnewz*. Retrieved May 28, 2006, from http://www.smallbusinessnewz.com/smallbusinessnewz-13-20030613ALittleFundMakesaBigMediaSplash.html

[45] Watson, T. J. (1963). *A business and its beliefs: The ideas that helped build IBM*. New York: McGraw-Hill. [McKinsey Foundation lecture series, Graduate School of Business, Columbia University]. [p. 5].

[46] Vaill, P. (1989). *Managing as a performing art: New ideas for a world of chaotic change*. San Francisco: Jossey Bass. [p. 223].

[47] Block, P. (1996). *Stewardship*. San Francisco: Berrett-Koehler.

[48] Monson, T. S. (1985). *Favorite quotations from the collection of Thomas S. Monson*. Salt Lake City, UT: Deseret Book Company.

[49] Barry, D. (2001, December 31). A man who became more than a mayor. *New York Times,* p. A.1.

[50] Senge, P. M. (1994). *The fifth discipline: The art and practice of the learning organization*. New York: Doubleday.

[51] Markides, C. C. (2000). *All the right moves: A guide to creating breakthrough strategy*. Boston: Harvard Business School Press.

[52] As cited in Haines, S. G. (1998). *The manager's pocket guide to systems thinking and learning*. Amherst, MA: HRD Press. [p. 175].

ARC Leadership Group is dedicated to advancing the study and practice of ethical leadership throughout the world by developing human potential, encouraging workplace excellence, and promoting positive transformation in organizational life. ARC advocates social responsibility, moral integrity, spiritual vitality, and authentic engagement among leaders everywhere.

Do you have a teachable leadership moment? If so, we'd like to hear about it. Send it to: P.O. Box 610986, San Jose, CA 95161. www.arcleadershipgroup.net

ISBN 141209964-1

9 781412 099646